Mental Health Reform

POINT COUNTERPOINT

Mental Health Reform

Alan Marzilli

SERIES CONSULTING EDITOR
Alan Marzilli, M.A., J.D.

CHELSEA HOUSE PUBLISHERS

A Haights Cross Communications Company

Philadelphia

This book is intended to serve only as a general introduction to the political and legal issues surrounding mental health reform. It is not intended as legal advice. If you have a legal problem, you should consult a licensed attorney who is familiar with the laws and procedures of your jurisdiction.

CHELSEA HOUSE PUBLISHERS

VP, New Product Development   Sally Cheney
Director of Production   Kim Shinners
Creative Manager   Takeshi Takahashi
Manufacturing Manager   Diann Grasse

Staff for MENTAL HEALTH REFORM

Editor   Patrick M.N. Stone
Production Editor   Jaimie Winkler
Photo Editor   Sarah Bloom
Series and Cover Designer   Keith Trego
Layout   21st Century Publishing and Communications, Inc.

A Haights Cross Communications ⚓ Company

http://www.chelseahouse.com

First Printing

1 3 5 7 9 8 6 4 2

Library of Congress Cataloging-in-Publication Data

Marzilli, Alan.
   Mental health reform/Alan Marzilli.
      p. cm.—(Point-counterpoint)
Includes bibliographical references and index.
   ISBN 0-7910-7372-6
   1. Insanity—Jurisprudence—United States—Juvenile literature. 2. Mental health laws—United States—Juvenile literature. 3. Mentally ill—Care—United States—Juvenile literature. [1. Insanity—Jurisprudence. 2. Mentally ill—Care.] I. Title. II. Series: Point-counterpoint (Philadelphia, Pa.)
KF480.Z9 M37 2002
344.73'044—dc21

                                                              2002015636

CONTENTS

Introduction

Alan Marzilli, M.A., J.D.
Durham, North Carolina

The debates presented in POINT/COUNTERPOINT are among the most interesting and controversial in contemporary American society, but studying them is more than an academic activity. They affect every citizen; they are the issues that today's leaders debate and tomorrow's will decide. The reader may one day play a central role in resolving them.

Why study both sides of the debate? It's possible that the reader will not yet have formed any opinion at all on the subject of this volume—but this is unlikely. It is more likely that the reader will already hold an opinion, probably a strong one, and very probably one formed without full exposure to the arguments of the other side. It is rare to hear an argument presented in a balanced way, and it is easy to form an opinion on too little information; these books will help to fill in the informational gaps that can never be avoided. More important, though, is the practical function of the series: Skillful argumentation requires a thorough knowledge of *both* sides—though there are seldom only two, and only by knowing what an opponent is likely to assert can one form an articulate response.

Perhaps more important is that listening to the other side sometimes helps one to see an opponent's arguments in a more human way. For example, Sister Helen Prejean, one of the nation's most visible opponents of capital punishment, has been deeply affected by her interactions with the families of murder victims. Seeing the families' grief and pain, she understands much better why people support the death penalty, and she is able to carry out her advocacy with a greater sensitivity to the needs and beliefs of those who do not agree with her. Her relativism, in turn, lends credibility to her work. Dismissing the other side of the argument as totally without merit can be too easy—it is far more useful to understand the nature of the controversy and the reasons *why* the issue defies resolution.

6

The most controversial issues of all are often those that center on a constitutional right. The Bill of Rights—the first ten amendments to the U.S. Constitution—spells out some of the most fundamental rights that distinguish the governmental system of the United States from those that allow fewer (or other) freedoms. But the sparsely worded document is open to interpretation, and clauses of only a few words are often at the heart of national debates. The Bill of Rights was meant to protect individual liberties; but the needs of some individuals clash with those of society as a whole, and when this happens someone has to decide where to draw the line. Thus the Constitution becomes a battleground between the rights of individuals to do as they please and the responsibility of the government to protect its citizens. The First Amendment's guarantee of "freedom of speech," for example, leads to a number of difficult questions. Some forms of expression, such as burning an American flag, lead to public outrage—but nevertheless are said to be protected by the First Amendment. Other types of expression that most people find objectionable, such as sexually explicit material involving children, are not protected because they are considered harmful. The question is not only where to draw the line, but how to do this without infringing on the personal liberties on which the United States was built.

The Bill of Rights raises many other questions about individual rights and the societal "good." Is a prayer before a high school football game an "establishment of religion" prohibited by the First Amendment? Does the Second Amendment's promise of "the right to bear arms" include concealed handguns? Is stopping and frisking someone standing on a corner known to be frequented by drug dealers a form of "unreasonable search and seizure" in violation of the Fourth Amendment? Although the nine-member U.S. Supreme Court has the ultimate authority in interpreting the Constitution, its answers do not always satisfy the public. When a group of nine people—sometimes by a five-to-four vote—makes a decision that affects the lives of hundreds of millions, public outcry can be expected. And the composition of the Court does change over time, so even a landmark decision is not guaranteed to stand forever. The limits of constitutional protection are always in flux.

These issues make headlines, divide courts, and decide elections. They are the questions most worthy of national debate, and this series aims to cover them as thoroughly as possible. Each volume sets out some of the key arguments surrounding a particular issue, even some views that most people consider extreme or radical—but presents a balanced perspective on the issue. Excerpts from the relevant laws and judicial opinions and references to central concepts, source material, and advocacy groups help the reader to explore the issues even further and to read "the letter of the law" just as the legislatures and the courts have established it.

It may seem that some debates—such as those over capital punishment and abortion, debates with a strong moral component—will never be resolved. But American history offers numerous examples of controversies that once seemed insurmountable but now are effectively settled, even if only on the surface. Abolitionists met with widespread resistance to their efforts to end slavery, and the controversy over that issue threatened to cleave the nation in two; but today public debate over the merits of slavery would be unthinkable, though racial inequalities still plague the nation. Similarly unthinkable at one time was suffrage for women and minorities, but this is now a matter of course. Distributing information about contraception once was a crime. Societies change, and attitudes change, and new questions of social justice are raised constantly while the old ones fade into irrelevancy.

Whatever the root of the controversy, the books in POINT/COUNTERPOINT seek to explain to the reader the origins of the debate, the current state of the law, and the arguments on both sides. The goal of the series is to inform the reader about the issues facing not only American politicians, but all of the nation's citizens, and to encourage the reader to become more actively involved in resolving these debates, as a voter, a concerned citizen, a journalist, an activist, or an elected official. Democracy is based on education, and every voice counts—so every opinion must be an informed one.

———————•————————•————————•———————

This volume examines the legal rights of a group of people who throughout history have had very few rights: people with mental illness. When the news media sensationalize an act of violence by someone with a history of psychiatric treatment, the public often calls for stronger laws for committing such people to hospitals. However, many question practices such as electroshock treatment, the physical restraining of patients, and involuntarily medicating patients with drugs that can have significant side effects.

In recent years, more and more people with mental illness have left the back wards of hospitals to lead fulfilling lives. While there is greater hope than ever before, questions remain about the best treatments and patients' right to decide for themselves what is best—as well as how the question of mental health care should be addressed by society as a whole. Mental illness affects millions of people in the United States, but the law is very unsettled, and tomorrow's leaders will have a huge impact on the debate.

Defining Mental Illness

The brain is the most complex part of the human body. Although medical science has been able to explain the inner workings of the heart, lungs, and digestive system, the workings of the brain remain—to a large extent—an unsolved mystery. As scientists struggle to explain how the brain works, they also seek to explain why the brain sometimes works in ways that it should not. What causes people to hear voices that do not exist? To develop crippling fears of the people around them? To feel so sad that they cannot get out of bed? Scientists are seeking answers to these questions so that they can better help people with mental illnesses.

The Tragedy of Kendra Webdale

For many people, mental illness is a time bomb that suddenly explodes, disrupting their lives and the lives of the people around them. Andrew Goldstein was just such a person. Growing up in

New York City, he had a promising future. He played on the tennis team and earned good grades at Bronx Science, one of the best public schools in the nation. But after a year at college, his bright future collapsed as he began to suffer the symptoms of schizophrenia, a serious mental illness. For the next decade, he would spend time in and out of the hospital, unable to work, hearing voices, and fearing that people were following him.

Have you, or has someone close to you, ever had to cope with a major illness or injury?

Like Andrew Goldstein, Kendra Webdale was another young person with great promise. As the year 1999 began, this bright, attractive woman from Buffalo was working in New York City, hoping to one day become a successful screenwriter. But on January 3, she and Andrew Goldstein met in a subway station, and what happened next would not only be a tragedy for these two young people and their families, but also would spark a national debate about the rights of people with mental illness.

Some of the people who stood on the subway platform remember a man behaving oddly. In New York City, it is common to see people with mental illness acting strangely, but Andrew Goldstein was unusually alarming, and people moved away from him as he approached. Just after 5:00 p.m., as the train rattled into the station, Goldstein asked an attractive young woman for the time. Before Kendra Webdale could answer, Goldstein suddenly pushed her in front of the train. Some witnesses said that it happened so quickly that Webdale did not even have a chance to scream before the oncoming train crushed her to death.

This horrible incident made headlines in New York and around the country, and soon many people were questioning the adequacy of our mental health systems. Since being diagnosed with schizophrenia, Goldstein had had a history of violence. He had attacked nurses, doctors, roommates, and strangers. But time after time, he had been released from hospitals to live on his own with very little medical attention. At the time of the Webdale killing, Goldstein was not taking the antipsychotic

medication that doctors had prescribed to control his hallucinations and delusions.

Many people used the "subway pusher" incident to argue that
society should be given more control over people with mental illness. In the wake of the tragedy, the New York state legislature
passed "Kendra's Law," which makes it easier to commit a person
with mental illness to a hospital against his or her will or to
require that a person comply with treatment while living in the
community (often called "involuntary outpatient commitment").
The supporters of the law argued that people with mental illnesses
are often too sick to realize that they need treatment.

On the other hand, many mental health advocates thought
that the problem was not that it was too difficult to force people
to undergo treatment, but that there are not enough services
available for people who need them. In the decade before he
killed Kendra Webdale, Goldstein had signed himself into
hospitals 13 times seeking treatment. Just six weeks earlier,
Goldstein had checked himself into a hospital, but his stay
had lasted only three weeks. Because insurance companies
pressure hospitals to reduce costs, patients are often released
before they are ready: Goldstein was released despite being
described by his psychiatrist as "disorganized, thought-disordered
. . . talking to himself . . . very delusional."[1]

The New York Times reported that Goldstein was released
with a week's worth of medication, but that nobody was
assigned to help ensure that he took his medications or returned
for any type of treatment: "This was like
a bad joke—that a man so sick, with his
history (of violence), would be sent into
the community with so little support."[2]
Around the nation, many supported the
need for greater funding for the treatment of schizophrenia and other mental
illnesses. Because good treatment can be quite expensive, many
people like Goldstein simply do not receive adequate treatment,
and often receive no treatment at all.

> **Do people have a right
> to take whatever steps
> necessary to make
> their neighborhoods
> feel safe?**

Surrounded by the family of Kendra Webdale, who was killed by a man with mental illness, New York's Governor George Pataki signs "Kendra's Law." The law lowers the standards for involuntarily committing someone to mental health treatment.

Andrew Goldstein's illness, schizophrenia, is one of a number of conditions classified as "mental illnesses" because they affect people's thoughts, moods, and behavior. However, many physicians and medical researchers now believe that most mental illnesses—like any other illnesses—have physical causes. Research has linked several mental illnesses to specific changes in the human brain or to the chemicals in the blood that act upon the brain.

Types of Mental Illness

Stories like Andrew Goldstein's reinforce the public's image of people with mental illness as violent, lazy, or antisocial. However, mental illnesses have a wide range of severity. Andrew Goldstein's condition is an example of mental illness at its worst; his symptoms prevented him from functioning normally as a member of society. However, there are a number of different mental illnesses, which differ in their symptoms, their level of impairment, and the effectiveness of their treatment.

Mental illnesses are much more common than you might think: Most people with mental illness either retain their ability to function or regain it with the help of medication, therapy, and other supports. According to the U.S. Surgeon General, nearly one out of every five Americans suffers from a mental illness each year. Among adults, 40 million people experience a mental illness each year; 6.5 million of these people have serious mental illness, which significantly disrupts their ability to work and do other everyday activities, and which requires intensive, ongoing treatment.

One of the most common forms of mental illness is depression, which is characterized by feelings of sadness, hopelessness, or irritability. Having these feelings occasionally is normal and does not necessarily mean that you are suffering from depression. However, a diagnosis of depression may be made when a person is significantly affected by these feelings for more than two weeks,

Major Types of Mental Illness

Depressive Disorders
1   Major Depressive Disorder
2   Dysthymic Disorder
3   Bipolar Disorder

Schizophrenia

Anxiety Disorders
1   Panic Disorder
2   Obsessive-Compulsive Disorder (OCD)
3   Post-Traumatic Stress Disorder (PTSD)
4   Generalized Anxiety Disorder (GAD)
5   Social Phobia
6   Agoraphobia and Specific Phobias

accompanied by other symptoms, such as fatigue, loss of appetite, difficulty sleeping, or inability to concentrate. Frequently, people suffering from depression have suicidal thoughts, and in serious or untreated cases, might act upon these thoughts.

Although depression can be serious, the good news is that it is also treatable. Often, mild to moderate depression (sometimes called "dysthymic disorder") is treated through counseling sessions. However, doctors usually treat more serious cases of depression—also called "major depression"—with medications called antidepressants. In 1988, Eli Lilly and Company created a revolution in the medical treatment of depression with the introduction of Prozac. Unlike previously available antidepressants, Prozac had relatively few side effects. Soon millions of Americans were taking Prozac, leading some critics to charge that doctors were prescribing it to people who did not really need it. However, the use of Prozac and similar drugs such as Paxil and Zoloft continues to be widespread.

Bipolar disorder (previously known as manic depression) involves many of the same symptoms of depression. However, a person with bipolar disorder also experiences periods of mania, an elevated mood that sharply contrasts with the feelings of depression. During manic episodes, a person might need very little sleep, talk extremely quickly, make unrealistic plans, or have an inflated sense of accomplishment or ability. Often, manic episodes also include harmful behaviors, such as spending sprees, drug or alcohol abuse, or sexual promiscuity. As with depression, bipolar disorder is usually treated with a combination of therapy and medication, specifically "mood stabilizers" such as lithium that help prevent and reduce both depression and mania. Depression and bipolar disorder are often called "mood disorders" because they affect the way that a person feels.

Worry and fear are normal human emotions, especially in the face of stressful situations like financial problems or a serious illness. However, some people experience excessive anxiety even when not facing something that most people would find stressful. Doctors have identified several different types of anxiety disorders that can be treated with therapy, medication, or both. People who suffer from generalized anxiety disorder, for example, worry excessively about everyday situations for more than six months and have unwanted effects from this worry, such as trouble sleeping, inability to concentrate, or muscle tension.

In contrast to the constant worry of generalized anxiety disorder, panic disorder strikes briefly but repeatedly. A panic attack is characterized by physical symptoms that are so intense that people often mistake panic attacks for heart attacks. Common symptoms include a racing heartbeat, sweating, shaking, dizziness, chest pain, and shortness of breath. People with panic disorder often experience these attacks when facing specific stressful situations, such as flying or being in a crowd.

Should society pay for treating people who have serious mental illness?

In obsessive-compulsive disorder (OCD), anxiety takes the form of repeated thoughts (obsessions) or repeated actions (compulsions) that interfere with everyday living. Some common examples of obsessions include being preoccupied with cleanliness or constantly worrying about having forgotten to do something. Compulsions involve acting out these obsessive thoughts, for example constantly washing the hands or checking to make sure that the stove is turned off.

Post-traumatic stress disorder (PTSD) is a common anxiety disorder among people who have been through extremely disturbing experiences such as sexual abuse or a serious accident. It is especially common among people who have been involved in battlefield combat—many veterans returning from wars were once said to be suffering from "shell shock." Doctors now know that traumatic experiences can lead to a wide variety of symptoms afterwards. A common symptom is a "flashback," during which a person momentarily believes that he or she is back in the stressful situation. Other symptoms might include nightmares or withdrawing from family and friends. Medication is not quite as effective for PTSD as it is for other anxiety disorders, such as

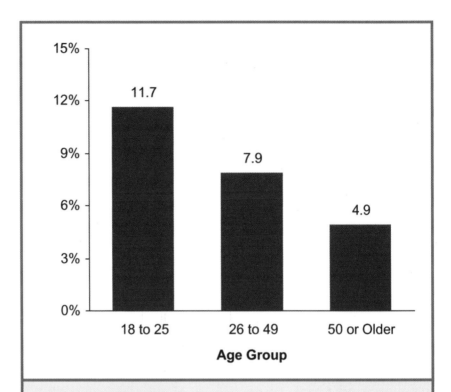

Percentages of adults (18+) who have had serious mental illness within the past year (2001), by age group. Serious mental illness is a very common problem. According to statistics provided by the U.S. Department of Health and Human Services, seven percent of adults in the United States experienced a mental illness during the year 2001. (*Serious mental illness* is defined as a diagnosable mental, behavioral, or emotional disorder that met criteria in the 4th edition of the *Diagnostic and Statistical Manual of Mental Disorders* [DSM–IV] and that resulted in functional impairment that substantially interfered with or limited one or more major life activities.)

generalized anxiety disorder, panic disorder, and OCD; however, the medical profession continues to develop therapies for PTSD and search for more effective medications.

Andrew Goldstein's illness, schizophrenia, is perhaps the most serious of the mental illnesses, not only for the patient, but also for the patient's family and for society at large. The National

Institute of Mental Health (NIMH), a federal research agency, describes schizophrenia as follows:

> Schizophrenia is a chronic, severe, and disabling brain disease. Approximately 1 percent of the population develops schizophrenia during their lifetime—more than 2 million Americans suffer from the illness in a given year.... People with schizophrenia often suffer terrifying symptoms such as hearing internal voices not heard by others, or believing that other people are reading their minds, controlling their thoughts, or plotting to harm them. These symptoms may leave them fearful and withdrawn. Their speech and behavior can be so disorganized that they may be incomprehensible or frightening to others. Available treatments can relieve many symptoms, but most people with schizophrenia continue to suffer some symptoms throughout their lives; it has been estimated that no more than one in five individuals recovers completely.[3]

Contrary to popular belief, schizophrenia does not involve a "split personality" like Dr. Jeckyll and Mr. Hyde. Rather, people experience symptoms—such as hearing voices and having unreasonable thoughts—that indicate a "break" from reality. Hallucinations are false sensory experiences, meaning that the patient hears, sees, feels, tastes, or smells something that is not really there. According to NIMH, "hearing voices that other people do not hear is the most common type of hallucination in schizophrenia. Voices may describe the patients' activities, carry on a conversation, warn of impending dangers, or even issue orders to the individual."[4]

Based on the statistics, is it likely that someone close to you has, or will develop, a mental illness?

The distorted thoughts experienced by a person with schizophrenia are called delusions. People with schizophrenia "often have delusions of persecution, or false and irrational beliefs that they are being cheated, harassed, poisoned, or conspired against.

. . . Sometimes the delusions experienced by people with schizo-phrenia are quite bizarre; for instance believing that a neighbor is controlling their behavior with magnetic waves; that people on television are directing special messages to them; or that their thoughts are being broadcast aloud to others."[5]

A number of antipsychotic medications exist to control hallucinations, delusions, and other "psychotic" symptoms, or distortions of the thought process. The first drugs to become available, such as Haldol and Thorazine, often have side effects that people think are worse than the illnesses they treat. For example, the older antipsychotic medications can cause perma-nent muscle twitches or partial paralysis in some people. More common, but less serious, side effects include dry mouth and weight gain. Recently, new "atypical" antipsychotic medications with fewer and less severe side effects have become available, but many people still suffer from complications.

The specific disorders listed above are some of the most common mental ill-nesses; however, many other conditions are classified as mental illnesses. Often, people show symptoms of more than one of these illnesses, and sometimes people can experi-ence great distress even if they do not fit into a specific category of mental illness. Other times, people are misdiagnosed with mental illnesses because physical illness can mimic the symptoms of mental illnesses.

How sad is sad enough to require professional help?

What would be the societal reasons for requiring someone to seek help?

What if a person with a serious mental illness posed no threat to anyone but refused treatment?

Fortunately, medical help is available for people with mental illnesses, and it is important to seek help if you or someone close to you might be suffering from a mental illness.

Treatments for Mental Illness

Many people devote their careers to helping people with mental illness. Psychiatrists are medical doctors who specialize in treating mental illnesses and can prescribe medications. Psychologists

Mental illness has been poorly understood throughout history, and it was once thought to be the result of demonic possession or, as in the case of Joan of Arc, the voices of the divine. Today, the causes of and most effective treatments for many kinds of mental illness remain elusive.

provide therapy or counseling but cannot prescribe medications. Social workers, often called case managers, help people with mental illnesses solve everyday problems, such as finding housing or accessing services. Many people who themselves have mental illnesses help others through self-help groups that are similar to Alcoholics Anonymous (AA).

If you were sick, would you want to take a medication that had serious side effects?

How bad would the side effects have to be to cause you to stop taking the medication?

By contrast, throughout history, people with mental illnesses have been ignored by society. Long ago, people with mental illness were thought to be possessed by demons. In Nazi Germany, people with mental illness were systematically killed. In the United States, until a few decades ago, most people with serious mental illnesses were kept locked in institutions. People lived in crowded conditions and were treated as less than human.

Although reformers like Dorothea Dix fought successfully for improvements, life in a mental institution remained bleak.

During the 1960s and 1970s, as science began to develop better medications for treating mental illness, many institutions closed or drastically reduced their numbers of patients. Unfortunately, as people were released from the hospitals into the community, too few services were created to serve people who had formerly been institutionalized. As a result, many people with mental illness became homeless, ended up in jail, lived in squalid conditions, or died from neglect.

After going from one extreme—institutionalizing people with mental illnesses—to another—neglecting them—many local and state governments looked for more effective ways to treat people with mental illnesses in the community. However, many advocates for people with mental illness feel that governments are still not doing enough. The trend toward community-based treatment has raised many questions about the rights of people with mental illness. When should a person be sent to a hospital? Who should determine what types of treatment a person receives? Perhaps most important, who should pay for these treatments?

Should people with serious mental illness be kept in hospitals indefinitely?

Who should decide when to release them, and how?

Despite the increased availability of effective treatments, mental illnesses such as schizophrenia, bipolar disorder, depression, and anxiety disorders continue to impose huge burdens on society. Events such as the killing of Kendra Webdale by schizophrenia patient Andrew Goldstein capture headlines, but because mental health treatments can be expensive and unpleasant, society continues to debate how much control a person should have over his or her own treatment, and who should pay for that treatment.

Inpatient and Outpatient Commitment Laws Are Not Strong Enough

W hen Andrew Goldstein pushed Kendra Webdale in front of a subway train in January 1999, the tragedy brought attention to a debate that had been simmering nationwide for many years. In fact, New York had been one of the major battlegrounds for debating laws that allow people to be involuntarily "committed" to treatment, whether in a hospital or in the community. Nationwide, commitment laws are generally limited to someone who is a danger to himself or herself, is a danger to other people, or is so "gravely disabled" that he or she cannot care for himself or herself.

Civil commitment laws should be broader to protect both individuals and society.

Commitment to a hospital or to outpatient treatment is usually a procedure covered by civil—as opposed to criminal—law. A person need not have violated any law to be committed, and the commitment does not result in a criminal record. However, because a commitment takes away a person's freedom, a person is entitled to a hearing to determine whether the commitment is valid. But because it is not a criminal proceeding, people do not have the same rights as those accused of a crime, such as the right to a trial by jury, or requirement that "guilt" be proven "beyond a reasonable doubt."

> **Can a person's freedom be taken away if she has not committed a crime?**

Many patients' rights advocates argue that the current laws are strong enough to protect individuals and society, while also protecting the civil liberties of people with mental illness. However, there is a growing movement of people who advocate for "assisted treatment" (broadening the standards for commitment) and "involuntary outpatient commitment" (requiring people to undergo treatment while living outside of a hospital). They point to incidents like the Webdale killing as support for their argument that current laws do not do enough to protect the safety and health of people with mental illnesses and society at large.

Ever since mental institutions began releasing large numbers of patients during the "deinstitutionalization" movement of the 1970s and 1980s, most people with serious mental illness have lived in the community, in a variety of conditions from acceptable to deplorable. Many people live in their own homes, but a significant number live in group homes, with overburdened family members, in run-down boarding homes, or on the streets.

Although community-based treatment has helped many people who would otherwise languish in state hospitals, others have not fared as well. Many people "fall through the cracks" of the system and receive no treatment or other support for their illnesses. As a result, a significant percentage of homeless people in the United States are people with serious mental illness. To many people, the solution to this problem is lowering the standard for committing someone to treatment, either in the hospital or under an involuntary outpatient commitment order, which requires the individual to comply with a treatment plan, usually involving medication, but does not require hospitalization so long as the individual complies with treatment.

The Treatment Advocacy Center (TAC) in Arlington, Virginia leads the push for expanding what it calls "assisted treatment," meaning involuntary treatment. In addition to the "danger to self or others" and "gravely disabled" standards, TAC's "Model Law for Assisted Treatment" would expand involuntary treatment to anyone who is "incapable of making an informed medical decision"—

> **Should people with serious mental illness be required to take medication?**
>
> **What does "serious" mean, and how "serious" would the illness have to be?**
>
> **What if the medication had "serious" side effects?**

> meaning that a person is unaware of the effects of his or her psychiatric disorder or that the person lacks the capacity to make a well-reasoned, willful, and knowing decision concerning his or her medical or psychiatric treatment. Any history of the person's non-compliance with treatment or of criminal acts related to his or her mental illness shall, if available, be considered.[1]

TAC's reason for wanting to lower the legal standard for committing someone to treatment, said its executive director, Mary Zdanowicz, in a June 2000 press release, is that because of current standards a person who needs treatment may "commit suicide, slowly die on a park bench from malnutrition or freezing temperatures, shoot someone or push a passerby into the path of an oncoming subway train" before he or she can be committed to treatment. "The legal standard should be need for treatment, not dangerousness alone," said Zdanowicz.

"Society has an obligation to save people from degradation, not just death."[2]

Answering critics who charge that the reason why people refuse treatment is that services are unavailable or inadequate, TAC president E. Fuller Torrey told *USA Today* that this is really due to a lack of awareness:

> You can . . . give out coffee and free cigarettes but people will not accept medication if they don't think they're sick. . . . That's why people with severe mental illness must be treated involuntarily.[3]

THE LETTER OF THE LAW

From Colorado's Civil Commitment Law:

(2) Any individual may petition the court in the county in which the respondent resides or is physically present alleging that there is a person who appears to be mentally ill and, as a result of such mental illness, appears to be a danger to others or to himself or appears to be gravely disabled and requesting that an evaluation of the person's condition be made.

(3) The petition for a court-ordered evaluation shall contain the following:

   (a) The name and address of the petitioner and his interest in the case;

   (b) The name of the person for whom evaluation is sought, who shall be designated as the respondent, and, if known to the petitioner, the address, age, sex, marital status, and occupation of the respondent;

   (c) Allegations of fact indicating that the respondent may be mentally ill and, as a result, a danger to others or to himself or gravely disabled and showing reasonable grounds to warrant an evaluation;

   (d) The name and address of every person known or believed by the petitioner to be legally responsible for the care, support, and maintenance of the respondent, if available;

   (e) The name, address, and telephone number of the attorney, if any, who has most recently represented the respondent. If there is no attorney, there shall be a statement as to whether, to the best knowledge of the petitioner, the respondent meets the criteria established by the legal aid agency operating in the county or city and county for it to represent a client.

27–10–106, C.R.S. (2002)

Some of the symptoms of mental illness do interfere with perceptions of reality, which can include a person's perception of his or her own illness; a person who does not realize that he or she has a mental illness is said to "lack insight." For example, someone with schizophrenia or bipolar disorder can have grandiose delusions, thinking that he or she has "special powers that are beyond those of the normal individual," or believing that he or she "is someone special, such as Jesus or the president."[4]

Have you ever been to see a physician you didn't like?

Would an offer of candy have changed your mind?

If people do not realize that they are ill, argue advocates for assisted treatment, then the answer is to force people into treatment. Without treatment, symptoms of mental illness can worsen. Although medications are not designed to "cure" mental illness, medication therapy can help reduce symptoms. Also, because many mental illnesses are periodic—meaning symptoms can get better or worse—medication therapy can help prevent symptoms from worsening. People with mental illness can suffer tremendously, not only from their symptoms, but also from the secondary effects of their illness, such as suicide, homelessness, victimization, and incarceration.

A key reason that people with serious mental illness should be forced into treatment, proponents of involuntary treatment argue, is that people who do not seek treatment are susceptible to suicide. Although someone who has suicidal thoughts and reveals them to a mental health professional can be committed to treatment under the "danger to self" standard, people often have strong suicidal feelings without revealing them. According to TAC:

> The consequences of requiring treatment to be withheld until a person becomes a danger to themselves is predictable. By that time, they are likely to be either one of the 19 percent (of people with serious mental illness) who attempt suicide or one of the 10 percent to 15 percent who eventually succeed.[5]

Since the 1960s, many people with mental illness have been released from mental hospitals, only to become homeless. Some advocates believe that homeless people with mental illness should be hospitalized involuntarily.

Many people with serious mental illness become homeless. Of the nation's approximately 450,000 homeless people, about one in three has a serious mental illness. Proponents of assisted treatment argue that the problem is the result of narrow commitment standards and that society has turned a blind eye on the plight of homeless people who have serious mental illness:

> Sadly, we have grown accustomed to public places dominated by wasted human forms huddled over steam grates for warmth in the winter. . . . The majority of homeless people regularly forage through garbage cans and dumpsters for food.[6]

Proponents of involuntary treatment believe that it can help protect people with serious mental illness from crime. A person with serious mental illness is nearly three times as likely to become a victim of violent crime than someone in the general population. In some groups, the statistics are even more alarming. One out of every three homeless women with serious mental illness will be the victim of one or more sexual assaults.

> **Will medical treatment help homeless people to find food?**
>
> **What about homeless people who do not have mental illness?**
>
> **How many homeless people are mentally ill?**

Another reason why many people advocate stronger civil commitment laws is that many people with serious mental illness end up violating criminal laws and being sentenced to jail or prison. In most major cities, the local jail is the facility that treats the largest number of people with serious mental illness, even though the jail may be poorly equipped to give proper care. New York mental health advocate D.J. Jaffe has argued that people who want to protect the civil liberties of people with serious mental illness ignore the fact that so many of them end up in jail or prison, with all of their civil rights taken away. "This population has been totally abandoned by those purporting to speak for the mentally ill," he said.[7]

> **Which would be more effective—requiring someone who has not committed a crime to undergo treatment, or providing better mental health services in prisons?**

Families need more options in committing people with mental illness.

In New York, the passage of Kendra's Law was due in part to the efforts of Kendra Webdale's surviving family members. However, in the nationwide push for broader commitment laws, many of the strongest advocates have not been the families of victims of violence, but people with spouses, parents, or adult sons or daughters with serious mental illness. Mental illness can create enormous burdens upon a family, far beyond the financial strain that expensive therapies and medications can create.

Often, caring for a family member with serious mental illness can become a full-time job. According to the U.S. Surgeon General:

> Family members of people with severe mental illnesses also encounter ignorance and stigma. Stigma translates into avoiding or blaming family members . . . Families also are under a great deal of stress associated with care giving and obtaining resources for their mentally ill members.
>
> Families—especially parents, siblings, adult children, and spouses—often provide housing, food, transportation, encouragement, and practical assistance. At the same time, schizophrenia and other mental disorders strain family ties. Symptoms of mental disorders may be disruptive and troubling, especially when they flare up. Even when there are no problems, living together can be stressful—interpersonally, socially, and economically. Parents and their adult children often perceive mental disorders and treatment differently, sometimes disagreeing about the best course of action.
>
> Consequently, families too have created support organizations. Some of these are professionally based and facilitated, often as part of a clinic or other treatment program. Others are peer run in the self-help model. Similar to self-help among people with mental illnesses, family self-help can range from small supportive groups to large organizations. The National Alliance for the Mentally Ill (NAMI) is the largest such organization.[8]

If a friend or family member had a serious mental illness and refused to take prescribed medication, what would you do?

What if the illness posed a threat to someone else? To you?

NAMI and many of its local and state chapters nation-wide have been supportive of broader commitment laws as a vehicle for providing help to people with serious mental ill-ness and easing the burden on families. Additionally, NAMI offers the "Family to Family" support program, which helps people cope more effectively with family members with mental illness.

Although supporters of broader commitment laws have stressed the benefits that such laws can have for people with mental illnesses and their families, it has been the public fear of violence that has most motivated the passage of laws such as Kendra's Law. Just months after the Webdale killing, another "subway pusher" aroused the fears of New Yorkers.

On April 28, 1999, Julio Perez, a homeless man with schizo-phrenia, pushed Edgar Rivera in front of an oncoming subway train. It was a scene eerily similar to that of the previous January. In the midst of a crowd of commuters during the evening rush hour, Perez was acting irrationally and frightening passengers; according to one witness, Perez punched his fist into the wall after another passenger asked him to move away. Then, without warning, Perez pushed Rivera in front of the oncoming train. Although the father of three survived, both of his legs were severed from his body by the weight of the train. It was later revealed that Perez had sought treatment from a hospital emergency room that very day but had been turned away.

> **Neither Perez nor Goldstein had been taking the prescribed medications, but would Kendra's law have prevented these tragedies?**

In announcing the passage of Kendra's law, New York Governor George Pataki stressed the need to protect the public from this type of incident. "We must ensure that mentally ill persons who are prone to violence adhere to the treatment programs they rely on to remain safe and stable members of their communities. . . . If they refuse to act responsibly by taking their medication, we must act to protect all New Yorkers."[9]

———————•———————•———————•———————

Supporters of "assisted treatment" argue that it should be easier to commit a person with mental illness to treatment, either in a hospital or in the community. They believe that because people often do not realize that they need mental health treatment, legal mechanisms are needed to prevent violence, suicide, and neglect.

Inpatient and Outpatient Commitment Laws Violate Rights

Across the nation, people with mental illness have joined together to fight for better conditions, much like the African-American civil rights movement and the women's movement have fought to end discrimination based upon race and gender. Many people with mental illness have joined advocacy groups, calling themselves either "consumers of mental health services," indicating that they are concerned with improving the quality of mental health services, or "psychiatric survivors," indicating that their experiences with the mental health system have caused them to believe that non-psychiatric alternatives are preferable.

One issue that has united many consumer/survivor advocacy groups nationwide is an opposition to the expansion of commitment laws, specifically opposing both broader standards for committing a person to treatment and involuntary outpatient commitment laws, which enable a court to order someone to comply with psychiatric treatment while living in the community. Many people have argued that current commitment laws—which allow commitment only in cases in which a person is a danger to himself or herself, is a danger to other people, or is so "gravely disabled" that he or she cannot care for himself or herself—are strong enough already.

> **Should a person with mental illness who is not dangerous be required to undergo treatment if it will improve his or her quality of life?**
>
> **Who should have the power to make that assessment?**
>
> **Can the same standards be applied to all people with mental illness?**

Commitment laws should not be broader.

Many advocates argue that laws like Kendra's Law—which allows the outpatient commitment of people who might not necessarily be dangerous but whose "lack of compliance with treatment for mental illness [has] at least twice in the last thirty-six months been a significant factor in necessitating hospitalization"[1]—go too far in restricting people's civil liberties. Many consumer/survivor groups and others have argued that such laws unfairly single out people with mental illness and deprive them of their freedom.

The U.S. Supreme Court has consistently held that the Constitution's promise of "due process" of law limits a state's ability to involuntarily commit a person with mental illness. For example, in *O'Connor v. Donaldson* (1975), the Court ruled unanimously that Florida's confinement of a man to a mental hospital was unfair because there was no evidence that he was dangerous:

> A finding of "mental illness" alone cannot justify a State's locking a person up against his will and keeping him indefinitely in simple custodial confinement. Assuming that that term can be given a reasonably precise content and that the "mentally ill" can be identified with reasonable accuracy, there is still no constitutional basis for confining such persons involuntarily if they are

Are there better reasons for confining people with mental illness, or is the Supreme Court's comparison fair?

dangerous to no one and can live safely in freedom.

May the State fence in the harmless mentally ill solely to save its citizens from exposure to those whose ways are different? One might as well ask if the State, to avoid public unease, could incarcerate all who are physically unattractive or socially eccentric.[2]

More recently, in *Kansas v. Crane*, the Court clarified its legal standard, holding that civil commitment laws are valid if

(1) the confinement takes place pursuant to proper procedures and evidentiary standards, (2) there is a finding of dangerousness either to one's self or to others, and (3) proof of dangerousness is coupled with the proof of some additional factor, such as a mental illness or mental abnormality.[3]

Commitment to mental health treatment—whether in a hospital or in the community—is an infringement upon personal choice. However, a state's infringement upon personal choice can be justified if an important state interest overrides a person's right to liberty. Proponents of expanded commitment laws argue that states have an important interest in providing treatment to people with serious mental illness, even if they do not fall into the "danger to self or others" or "gravely disabled" categories. Opponents believe that individual choice must be respected in cases in which the individual poses no threat to anyone.

Rather than expanding the criteria for commitment, many people argue that committing someone to treatment should be made more difficult. Many advocates charge that even under the current system, the rights of people with mental illness are violated on a regular basis. In addition to limiting the circumstances under which a person can be committed, constitutional due process also requires that people who are involuntarily

Under most circumstances, people can only be jailed for past actions, but during World War II many Japanese-Americans were detained because they were thought to be a threat. Today, a person with mental illness can be held in a locked facility if a judge determines that the person poses a threat to others.

committed to treatment receive a hearing before a judge. Typically, at a commitment hearing, a mental health professional presents a psychiatric assessment, and the patient also has—or should have—the opportunity to testify.

However, the legal theory protecting the rights of individuals with mental illness, many say, does not reflect the bleak reality of our court system. Regardless of any protections that may technically be provided by laws and the Constitution, critics charge, civil commitment hearings do little to protect people's rights. In

When an attorney disagrees with his or her client, whose position should the attorney present in court?

What if the client has mental illness?

practice, reports law professor Bruce Winick, judges tend to agree with the psychiatric testimony about 95 percent of the time, and in some places 100 percent of the time. Winick attributes these statistics to a lack of vigorous representation by patients' attorneys: "Many attorneys relax their advocacy role and adopt a 'paternalistic' or 'best interests' approach, in which they seek to implement what [the attorneys] may perceive as their clients' best interests."[4] The result, states Winick, is a "farce" hearing in which judges merely "rubber-stamp" the psychiatrists' recommendations. The patient's viewpoint is often completely ignored.

Many critics of expanded commitment laws argue that because the civil commitment process is so biased against people with mental illnesses, families and doctors are able to misuse the commitment process and commit people for the wrong reasons. Doctors might seek a commitment order simply to gain more control in the relationship or, even worse, to generate more business. Families might have family members with mental illness committed to a hospital simply to give the family a break from caring for the person.

In an interview with *The Psychiatric Times*, psychiatrist Dan Creson gave real-life examples of how the commitment process has been misused. Creson charged that doctors have committed their patients to hospitals simply because the patients had started smoking more frequently. He also reported that one family had their daughter committed to a hospital under the pretense that she needed treatment, but their real motivation was that the daughter was dating someone of a different race.[5]

> **What if you had an illness that enabled your family to imprison you whenever you did something "wrong"?**

Because people with mental illness have not been successful at organizing themselves as a civil rights movement, concluded law professors John La Fond and Mary Durham, family members have been very successful in encouraging legislators to enact stronger broader commitment laws. "Families thus became 'advocates' for the mentally ill, effectively masking the conflict of interest between those mentally ill citizens who wanted to stay out of psychiatric facilities and family members who wanted them hospitalized."[6] As a result, much mental health "advocacy" does not completely reflect the views of people with mental illness.

Broader standards are based on misconceptions about mental illness.

Opponents of expanded commitment laws charge that such laws are passed based on misguided public fears of people with mental illness. For example, Kendra's Law in New York was passed at a time of public outrage against the "subway pushers." However, most people with mental illness are not violent. In fact, a research study by the MacArthur Foundation found that people with mental illness—if they do not abuse drugs and alcohol—are no more violent than the general population.[7] Substance abuse is a much more significant factor in determining whether someone will be violent than mental illness is.

Many advocates think that the media plays a large role in the public's misperception that people with mental illness are violent. All too often, when television, radio, and newspapers report crimes, they announce whether the person responsible has a "history of mental illness." Many advocates think that such reporting is unfair and—like reporting a criminal suspect's race—reinforces public stereotypes. As a result, many advocates pressure news sources not to highlight the psychiatric history of people charged with violent crimes.

Should news organizations be encouraged to withhold factual information in the interest of reducing prejudice?

Should someone have the power to control the media in order to send a certain message to the public?

Even though some people with mental illnesses are violent, many advocates question the fairness of singling out people with mental illness for commitment even if they have done nothing illegal. Other groups of people who are prone to violence are not subject to civil commitment. For example,

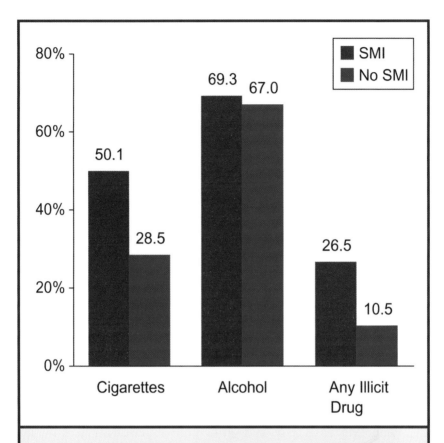

Percentages of adults (18+) who reported substance use within the past year (2001), by substance. Substance use is unfortunately very widespread among people with serious mental illness (SMI), and it can lead to misconceptions and stereotypes that impede efforts to increase public support. Addiction often complicates treatment and results in legal problems. (*Serious mental illness* is defined as a diagnosable mental, behavioral, or emotional disorder that met criteria in the 4th edition of the *Diagnostic and Statistical Manual of Mental Disorders* [DSM–IV] and that resulted in functional impairment that substantially interfered with or limited one or more major life activities. *Any illicit drug* refers to marijuana/hashish; cocaine, including crack; inhalants; hallucinogens; heroin; or any prescription-type drug used nonmedically.)

street gang members, alcoholics and drug addicts, high school dropouts, and young men living in low-income neighborhoods might all be much more likely than the average person to commit a violent crime. Different racial and ethnic groups have different rates of violent crime. However, under our legal system, a person generally cannot be detained simply for being in a group of people who might be more violent. Motorcycle gang members can ride down the highway wearing clothing that announces their gang affiliation. And today, people look with horror on the practice of detaining Japanese-Americans during World War II based on fears that they would aid Japan in its war against the United States.

Should society be able to detain gang members in order to prevent crime?

In general, somebody must commit a violent crime before he or she can be detained. However, a person who is perceived as dangerous due to a mental illness can be detained to prevent violence. By contrast, even though substance abuse is a much greater predictor of violence, a person generally cannot be required to undergo treatment for drug and alcohol abuse, unless he or she has been convicted of a crime or agrees to a treatment program in order to avoid criminal charges.

It is important to note that a person with mental illness can be committed to treatment on the basis of being a danger to himself or herself, even though society rarely takes away an adult's individual liberty in the name of protection from other forms of illness. Drug or alcohol abuse also poses a risk to the individual, but this cannot serve as the basis for committing someone to treatment. People with other illnesses are allowed to make poor choices. For example, a court cannot order a person with the debilitating lung disease emphysema to quit smoking. Nor can a court order a person with heart disease to lose weight, or a person with diabetes to stop eating candy.

The courts have long recognized a general right to refuse

unwanted medical treatment. Although a court can order psychiatric treatment, a court certainly cannot order a person with diabetes to take insulin. As described by U.S. Supreme Court Justice Brennan in the case of *Cruzan v. Director, MDH*—the MDH being the Missouri Department of Health—"The right to be free from unwanted medical attention is a right to evaluate the potential benefit of treatment and its possible consequences according to one's own values and to make a personal decision whether to subject oneself to the intrusion."[8]

> **Should states have the power to require people to undergo medical treatment?**
>
> **Should people be kept on life support who have no hope of recovery?**
>
> **What does "recovery" mean in this context?**

However, the right to refuse treatment can be overridden in instances in which the person is not competent to make a medical decision. In the case of Nancy Cruzan, who was in a vegetative state—a deep and evidently permanent coma—following a serious car accident, the Court found that the state could require "clear and convincing evidence" that Cruzan would have wished to refuse the feeding and breathing tubes that kept her alive. Many people believe that commitment laws are based on an erroneous assumption that people with mental illness are incompetent to make their own decisions. Ironically, Andrew Goldstein, whose killing of Kendra Webdale led to New York's involuntary outpatient commitment laws, was found competent to stand trial, and the jury rejected his insanity plea.

Involuntary outpatient commitment laws are not necessary.

Of particular concern to consumer/survivor activists is involuntary outpatient commitment. Many other advocates share this concern. The National Association of Protection and Advocacy

Systems used the following scenario to call into question the fairness of involuntary outpatient commitment:

> Imagine that you are sitting home watching television with your family. You hear a knock at your door and think it is odd that someone is knocking this late at night. You answer the door and it's a police officer coming to take you to a psychiatric hospital. You have not hurt anyone. Your family is safe and happy. The only "crime" you committed was that you did not want to continue to live with the side effects of Lithium and you chose to stop taking the drug prescribed for your bipolar disorder.[9]

In addition to civil libertarian arguments, one of the strongest arguments against expanded involuntary commitment laws, and in particular involuntary outpatient commitment laws, is that there is no solid evidence that involuntary outpatient commitment works. When asked by the California legislature to review available research about the effectiveness of involuntary outpatient commitment laws in other states, the RAND Corporation, a nonprofit research organization, concluded—after examining factors such as hospitalization rates, arrests, psychiatric symptoms, violence, and homelessness—that "the empirical literature does not tell us whether a court order is necessary to achieve good outcomes."[10]

According to the RAND Corporation, the problem with existing studies that conclude that involuntary outpatient commitment is effective was that in each case where outpatient commitments had a positive effect, the person had access to a wide variety of mental health services in the community. Typically, a person with mental illness does not have access to

If a mental health system has limited resources, should those resources be used to treat those people who are most likely to commit violent acts? Or some other group?

How can administrators tell who is most likely to commit a violent act?

proper care on a voluntary basis: Remember that Andrew Goldstein had repeatedly sought mental health care but was turned away for various reasons.

Opponents of expanded commitment laws argue that it is

THE LETTER OF THE LAW

From "Kendra's Law":

A patient may be ordered to obtain assisted outpatient treatment if the court finds that:

(1) the patient is eighteen years of age or older; and

(2) the patient is suffering from a mental illness; and

(3) the patient is unlikely to survive safely in the community without supervision, based on a clinical determination; and

(4) the patient has a history of lack of compliance with treatment for mental illness that has:

    (i)   at least twice within the last thirty-six months been a significant factor in necessitating hospitalization in a hospital, or receipt of services in a forensic or other mental health unit of a correctional facility or a local correctional facility, not including any period during which the person was hospitalized or incarcerated immediately preceding the filing of the petition or;

    (ii) resulted in one or more acts of serious violent behavior toward self or others or threats of, or attempts at, serious physical harm to self or others within the last forty-eight months, not including any period in which the person was hospitalized or incarcerated immediately preceding the filing of the petition; and

(5) the patient is, as a result of his or her mental illness, unlikely to voluntarily participate in the recommended treatment pursuant to the treatment plan; and

(6) in view of the patient's treatment history and current behavior, the patient is in need of assisted outpatient treatment in order to prevent a relapse or deterioration which would be likely to result in serious harm to the patient or others as defined in section 9.01 of this article; and

(7) it is likely that the patient will benefit from assisted outpatient treatment....

—New York State Consolidated Laws: Mental Hygiene: §9.60

illogical to pass laws that require people to comply with treatment when there are simply not enough treatment options available to people in the community. In the wake of the deinstitutionalization movement of past decades, in which many state hospitals were closed or downsized, states generally have not reinvested the money saved in creating community-based mental health services. The result, many mental health advocates say, is a system in which people with mental illness are likely to end up homeless or in jail because they do not have access to the care that they need.

The International Association of Psychosocial Rehabilitation Services, an organization that represents community-based mental health care providers, criticized involuntary outpatient commitment in an official policy statement:

> Court ordered involuntary outpatient commitment holds no promise of more or better care for anyone—not for those committed or those seeking services voluntarily. IOC will do little to increase the availability of services where they do not exist or are inadequate. In fact, the passage of involuntary outpatient commitment laws will be a false panacea, which hides the real need—appropriate funding for mental health services.[11]

In an era in which many states are cutting mental health budgets, this debate is certain to continue.

Opponents of involuntary treatment contend that current standards—which limit commitment to cases involving "danger to self or others" or "grave disability"—are sufficient to protect society while respecting the rights of people with mental illness. Expanding the standards of commitment would open the system to abuse, and it is fundamentally unfair to restrain the liberty of a person who has not committed a crime. The real problem, opponents say, is a lack of services in the community.

Doctors, Hospitals, and Family Members Need More Control Over the Treatment of People with Mental Illness

O pinion polls conducted among doctors reveal that it is an extremely frustrating time to practice medicine. Increasingly, doctors' ability to treat their patients is curtailed by restrictions imposed by managed care companies, such as Health Maintenance Organizations (HMOs), which seek to control medical costs by placing limits on the types of care that doctors provide. These restrictions can be especially significant in psychiatric care. Many managed care companies, for example, limit the number of visits a person can make to a psychiatrist in a year, limit the length of the visits to 15 minutes rather than the typical hour, and dictate which medications a doctor can or

> **Should anyone other than a patient and that patient's doctor be allowed to make decisions that affect that patient's health care?**

cannot prescribe. Doctors and citizens have both fought for laws that would eliminate these restrictions, but opponents say such restrictions are needed to control skyrocketing health care costs.

Deinstitutionalization has resulted in too little control over treatment.

In the 1960s and 1970s, while many people were being released from state mental hospitals, patient advocates fought for and won broader rights for people with mental illness. It was in the wake of the deinstitutionalization movement that states made their commitment standards narrower: no longer was a psychiatrist's opinion enough to commit someone to the hospital; a person had to be dangerous or gravely disabled, as determined by a judge. La Fond and Durham concluded that many psychiatrists perceived these restrictive new laws as threatening because commitment hearings are time-consuming and because "time spent in court was time not spent seeing patients, harmful both professionally and financially."[1] As homelessness continues to increase and violent incidents capture headlines, these standards have been hotly debated.

Many psychiatrists contend that patient advocates are too concerned with patients' civil liberties and not concerned enough with their overall well-being. Some critics of patients' rights advocates have charged that their opponents would prefer to see their clients "die with their rights on"—implying that laws restricting involuntary care cause people who are unaware that they could benefit from treatment to die from neglect. One California police officer asked *USA Today*, "Has the pendulum swung so far that people have the right to die from some disease? To be eaten by rats in some alley?"[2]

> **How should doctors handle patients who become violent?**
>
> **What special dangers might there be in such violence?**

Like restrictive commitment laws, many other laws that some people view as reforms in mental health rights have caused other people to wonder whether the United States has gone too far in protecting individual rights. Examples include confidentiality laws, which often shut family members out of treatment decisions, and laws restricting certain types of treatment. Many have questioned whether laws that were designed to protect individual rights are actually harming people with mental illness by preventing doctors, hospitals, and family members from ensuring that people get the care that they need for their illness.

Generally, even if a person has a mental illness, he or she has the right to make his or her own decisions, unless a court has declared him or her incompetent. Many doctors, family members of people with mental illness, police officers, and even some people who themselves have mental illness question this standard, believing that serious mental illness renders people incapable of making decisions that are in their own best interest.

Often, people with mental illness deny that they are sick: psychiatrists call this a "lack of insight." For example, people experiencing psychosis might truly believe that they are someone famous and that *everyone else around them* is crazy. When people are manic, they might believe that they have special powers rather than an illness.

Should people who suffer from delusions or hallucinations be able to make their own health care decisions?

Electroconvulsive therapy should not be unnecessarily restricted.

One of the most controversial treatments in psychiatry—perhaps in all of medicine—is a procedure that the medical profession calls electroconvulsive therapy (ECT) but many former patients call "shock treatment." Used most frequently on patients suffering from severe depression that has not responded to treatment with medication, ECT involves stimulating the brain with electrical currents. First, the patient is given general anesthesia, which—also used for surgery—causes temporary unconsciousness; and muscle relaxants, which help to prevent uncontrolled movements during the procedure. Next, electrodes are attached to the patient's head and an electrical current is sent through the patient's brain. The result is a seizure, similar to an epileptic seizure.

Nobody is sure exactly why or how ECT works, but the American Psychiatric Association, the American Medical Association, and international doctors' groups tout ECT as an effective treatment for severe depression, mania associated with bipolar disorder, and psychosis associated with schizophrenia. Additionally, the doctors' groups say, ECT's side effects are few, mild, and rare; therefore, ECT is particularly useful for treating people who are elderly or who have medical illnesses.

However, many hospitals do not use ECT, and numerous states have laws regulating its use—some doctors find these restrictions to be particularly frustrating. Part of the problem, according to the American Psychiatric Association, is that the public has a very negative opinion of ECT, and that "ECT is frightening to many people, thanks in part to its depiction in the film *One Flew Over the Cuckoo's Nest.*"[3] This film won the 1975 Academy Award for best picture for its portrayal of the horrible conditions in a mental hospital. Because many people saw the movie, it was influential in shaping public opinion about psychiatric treatment and helped provide support to patients' rights legislation. However, ECT supporters argue, the public's view of the procedure is based on antiquated perceptions, and ECT is very different today.

> **Is the fact that "shock treatment" is still in use common knowledge?**
>
> ***Should*** **this therapy still be in use?**

Doctors' efforts to administer ECT have been particularly hampered by the work of consumer/survivor activists, who have worked for state laws restricting ECT and who have put pressure on hospitals to discontinue the procedure. According to the American Psychiatric Association,

> [s]ome people who advocate legislative bans against ECT are former psychiatric patients who have undergone the procedure and believe that they have been harmed by it and that the treatment is used to punish patients' misbehavior and make them more docile. This is untrue.[4]

Even in places where ECT is used, a result of the controversy is that the procedures for "informed consent" require that the procedure be explained in detail and that written permission be obtained from the patient (or from a designated family member if a court has found the patient to be incompetent to make his or her own decisions).

Who has a better understanding of ECT—doctors who have studied and administered it many times, or patients who have experienced it a few times?

The basic controversy surrounding ECT is that some, but not all, doctors and former patients disagree about the safety and effectiveness of the procedure; many doctors, and the organizations that represent them, believe that physicians should be allowed to exercise their professional judgment as to what is best for their patients, without interference from what they see as unnecessary and uninformed rules and regulations.

Seclusion and restraints should not be unnecessarily restricted.

Another area in which there has been considerable controversy between doctors' groups and patient advocates has been the use of seclusion and restraints. To some people, these words conjure images of "rubber rooms" and strait-jackets. However, many health care professionals believe that in order to maintain safety and treat patients effectively they must be allowed to isolate patients from other patients or sometimes physically restrain them when they become violent. However, to the dismay of doctors' groups, patient advocates

THE LETTER OF THE LAW

From federal law on restraint and seclusion:

Restraints and seclusion may only be imposed … if—

(1) the restraints or seclusion are imposed to ensure the physical safety of the resident, a staff member, or others; and

(2) the restraints or seclusion are imposed only upon the written order of a physician, or other licensed practitioner permitted by the State and the facility to order such restraint or seclusion, that specifies the duration and circumstances under which the restraints are to be used (except in emergency circumstances specified by the Secretary until such an order could reasonably be obtained)….

The term "restraints" means—

(A) any physical restraint that is a mechanical or personal restriction that immobilizes or reduces the ability of an individual to move his or her arms, legs, or head freely, not including devices, such as orthopedically prescribed devices, surgical dressings or bandages, protective helmets, or any other methods that involve the physical holding of a resident for the purpose of conducting routine physical examinations or tests or to protect the resident from falling out of bed or to permit the resident to participate in activities without the risk of physical harm to the resident (such term does not include a physical escort); and

(B) a drug or medication that is used as a restraint to control behavior or restrict the resident's freedom of movement that is not a standard treatment for the resident's medical or psychiatric condition….

The term "seclusion" means a behavior control technique involving locked isolation.

— 42 U.S.C. §290ii

have used highly publicized deaths to lobby for greater restrictions on the use of seclusion and restraints.

The issue of the use of seclusion and restraints captured national attention in 1998, when *The Hartford Courant* ran a series of articles charging that hundreds of people nationwide had died while in restraints or seclusion. As a result, a number of patients' rights advocates pressured Congress to limit the use of restraints and seclusion. Some advocates pressed for a standard that allowed their use only for the safety of the patient, while others pressed for a complete ban on the practices. While making it clear that they believed that seclusion and restraints should not be used in a way that leads to patients' deaths, the American Psychiatric Association (APA) opposed the legislation before Congress:

Do you think that the government should protect people from jeopardizing their own health?

Should there be restrictions on riding a motorcycle without a helmet? Smoking? Being overweight?

As clinicians, we believe that the ultimate responsibility of the decision to seclude or restrain the individual patient must rest with the treating psychiatrist. Well-intentioned law and regulation are at best a crude instrument that cannot be a substitute for individual clinical expertise. [5]

In the opinion of the doctors' group, laws that are based on public outcry about isolated incidents and that take decisions out of doctors' hands have a negative impact on patient care.

The APA warned Congress that—in an era in which people are hospitalized only in times of crisis, when they are most likely to be violent—limiting the use of seclusion and restraints would have an overall negative impact on the health and safety of patients. The group testified that restraint was the best way to care for more extreme cases:

> [W]e are treating sicker patients in shorter time and in more acute stages of their illness. This population is one in which—regardless of what one may feel about restraints or seclusion—we simply cannot allow our distaste for the intervention to take the place of clinical judgment.[6]

Finding a compromise between the positions of the doctors' group and the patients' rights advocates, Congress ultimately passed legislation banning any facility receiving federal funding from using seclusion and restraints "for purposes of discipline and convenience" and allowing their use only "to ensure the physical safety of the resident, a staff member, or others."[7] However, many psychiatrists remained concerned that "well-intentioned but inflexible bureaucratic regulations"[8] would interfere with their ability to practice medicine.

People with mental illness should follow their doctors' advice.

Many physicians are also somewhat cautious about reforms that seek to make people with mental illness "equal partners" in their treatment. Ethical obligations require psychiatrists to provide information to their patients about their illness, treatment, and treatment alternatives so that a patient can give consent to the treatment plan. However, some psychiatrists believe that people whose thought processes are impaired do not really have the capacity to make informed choices

> **Should patients have a say in their treatment, or should they just follow the advice of doctors?**

about their treatment and should therefore follow their physician's advice.

Many doctors are concerned that too much misinformation is spread about mental illness. Psychiatrist Sally Satel is particularly concerned that radical consumer/ survivors are having a negative impact on patient care. She acknowledges that in the past, doctors prescribed antipsychotic medications in doses that are now considered too high, and that older antipsychotic medications caused significant side effects. However, Satel writes, "dosing schedules are more refined, and the new antipsychotic drugs produce fewer disabling side effects," and therefore some consumer/survivors are "fighting an image of pharmacotherapy that no longer applies."[9] Satel's major concern is that a small number of radical consumer/survivors are compromising the health and safety of people with mental illness through public misinformation and influencing legislation: in effect, she believes, the activists are "fighting against policies that can help thousands who are far sicker than they are."[10]

The media and the Internet can also be sources of misleading information about many issues, especially alternative treatments that doctors do not believe are effective.

What lends credibility to information heard on the news or read on the Internet?

Frequently, an alternative treatment— such as using the herb St. John's Wort for depression or using megadoses of vitamins for schizophrenia—becomes popular based on media reports or information shared on the Internet before there is any real scientific data demonstrating whether or not the treatment is effective. While some doctors believe that it is desirable for patients to investigate alternative therapies, many others believe that allowing patients to have too much influence over their own treatment can lead to ineffective or even dangerous results.

It should be easier to obtain treatment for a family member with mental illness.

Like physicians, family members of people with mental illnesses often want to exercise more control over the treatment of their loved ones with mental illness. In the wake of the closing and downsizing of state mental hospitals, and because widespread unemployment among people with serious mental illness limits housing options, many live with family members. In many households, this creates a stressful environment, which "often becomes a real-life horror movie that siphons away savings accounts, grinds away at family relations and leaves [family members] exhausted and at odds with doctors, judges and the police."[11] Laws that were designed to protect the rights of individuals create tensions among families. Because families frequently devote a great deal of energy and effort to caring for people with mental illness, and often accept responsibility for the costs of treatment, some caregivers are frustrated by laws that limit their involvement in their family member's mental health treatment.

Because of commitment laws that limit a family's ability to force a relative into treatment, too often it is only after the police get involved that people receive any treatment for their mental illness. The case of Rodger Gambs, a California man with schizophrenia, and his parents illustrates this problem. Believing that aliens had invaded his house, Gambs began abusing drugs and alcohol. He was arrested numerous times for minor crimes such as trespassing and vagrancy, and although his parents

> **Should a person with a mental illness be allowed to own a gun if she is unusually afraid of aliens? Vampires? Conspiracy?**

begged the court system repeatedly to force him into treatment, he was never committed because he was not thought to be dangerous. Even after he took two guns from a locked closet to scare away "vampires" in the back yard, the court would not commit him to treatment. Desperate, his parents pressed theft charges against him (for taking the guns), and it was only after pleading "not guilty by reason of insanity" that Gambs was committed to a hospital for treatment. His mother told USA Today, "No one should have to go through what we went through."[12]

The Gambs family's experience is not an isolated one. An Alabama woman whose son has mental illness expressed her frustration at a similar situation: "Instead of being placed in a supportive environment . . . my son was placed in the county jail. . . . [T]o someone suffering from the acute phase of a mental illness, the horror of such an experience is greatly magnified in its devastation and is frequently life threatening."[13]

Not only do family members often feel left out of the decision-making process when it comes to seeking treatment, families often know very little about the treatment that a person does receive. State laws, as well as doctors' own code of professional ethics, prevent doctors from releasing information about adults to their family members except in very limited circumstances. Revealing information to family members is permitted if the person consents to the information's being shared or if a court determines that the person is incompetent to make his or her own medical decisions. Additionally, if a person reveals an intent to harm a family member, a psychiatrist can reveal this threat to the family. Often, families express frustration that they cannot find out information about the diagnosis and treatment of family members with mental illness.

> **When should a minor patient's family lose access to that patient's medical records?**

Treating any illness can be a balancing act. Although doctors make recommendations about treating illnesses, patients often disagree with their doctors, seek second opinions, or simply ignore their doctors' advice. However, many people believe that the impairment of reasoning caused by mental illness, coupled with the possibility of violence or suicide, justifies increased control over the treatment of people with mental illness.

Many people believe that society has gone too far in protecting individual rights and has taken control of mental health treatment out of the hands of doctors and family members, who are better able to make decisions for people with mental illness. Doctors' groups feel that restrictions on the use of electroconvulsive therapy, restraints, and seclusion hamper their ability to provide effective treatment. Family members feel helpless in trying to get help for their loved ones with mental illness.

People with Mental Illness Need More Control Over Their Own Treatment

The fundamental flaw of today's mental health system, many believe, is that people with mental illness are denied the right to make their own decisions. In America today, most adults have the right to make their own decisions, whether good or bad; exceptions include prisoners and people who have been declared legally incompetent to make their own decisions. Under current notions of liberty, it seems almost inconceivable that the government would ban adults from smoking cigarettes or try to keep overweight people from eating fast food. Civil libertarians push for even less government control over people's lives; many advocate for the legalization of marijuana or the abolition of motorcycle helmet laws, for example.

It also seems unquestionable that a competent adult has the right to have control over his or her own medical treatment.

Legally speaking, this right is grounded both in the Fourteenth Amendment's "due process" clause and in centuries of common-law court decisions. Benjamin Cardozo, who would later become a Supreme Court justice, once wrote, "Every human being of adult years and sound mind has a right to determine what shall be done with his own body, and a surgeon who performs an operation without his patient's consent commits an assault."[1]

> **How would you feel if you were locked in a room or otherwise restrained even though you had not committed a crime?**
>
> **Why might this happen?**

Psychiatric patients should have the same rights as other patients.

The doctrine of "informed consent" requires that a doctor tell his or her patients all of the risks and benefits of a particular treatment and then let the patient decide whether to accept the treatment. (An obvious exception is providing emergency medical care to an unconscious person.) In addition to the decision whether or not to have surgery, a person's right to control his or her own treatment can also include a decision whether or not to undergo a particular regimen of chemotherapy that might have a small chance of curing cancer but certainly will cause extensive and painful side effects. A cancer patient also has the right to decide whether or not to take an experimental drug with unproven effectiveness or side effects, as well as the right to decide whether or not to participate in a medical research study.

By contrast—to the dismay of many mental health advocates—the wishes of many people with mental illness are ignored, and they are forced to undergo treatment through the involuntary commitment process. Other times, people are coerced into accepting treatments that they would not themselves choose. For example, a treatment program in Wisconsin has withheld Social Security checks from its clients until they agreed to receive an injection of an antipsychotic medication. Many radical patients' rights activists call for outright bans of such practices as electroconvulsive therapy (ECT), restraint and seclusion, and even the use of psychiatric medications. Activists taking a more moderate position call for strengthening the right of informed consent for people with mental illness and providing more resources to enforce that right.

Electroconvulsive therapy should be banned or highly restricted.

The problem with today's mental health system, many advocates assert, is that many treatments can cause more harm than good, either through emotional trauma or actual physiological damage to the brain. Although medicine has abandoned the lobotomy—removing a portion of the brain in an effort to "cure" mental illness—many treatments still in use can be quite traumatic. A frequent target of criticism is ECT; despite the medical community's claim that the procedure is safe and effective, many people who have undergone the procedure question both its effectiveness and its safety.

Can a state employee effectively represent a person's complaints against the state?

Self-proclaimed "shock survivors" have started public education campaigns, including websites, to share their experiences and opinions. Many believe that the process of jolting a person's brain with electricity is barbaric and dehumanizing, and they maintain that the procedure can cause permanent brain damage, including significant memory loss. Liz Spikol, a newspaper columnist who underwent ECT in 1996, writes, "I have a severely compromised memory for the years—years—between 1986 and 1998." Based on her experiences and research on the subject, she concludes, "I don't believe ECT had any long-term benefit for me, or as studies have shown, for any psychiatric patient."[2]

Many other advocates question whether the medical community as a whole misrepresents ECT and whether individual doctors misrepresent ECT when discussing it with patients. Many advocates have expressed concern that doctors misrepresent the danger of memory loss when discussing the procedure with patients, and perhaps more alarmingly, misrepresent the risks of death or injury to elderly patients, who more frequently receive the treatments than younger patients. The National Mental Health Association, a mainstream advocacy group, has taken the following position:

> [P]otential ECT recipients and their significant others, and families or guardians when appropriate, must have access to information on the procedure from a range of sources, both pro and con, to enable them to make truly informed decisions about it. Most important, anyone who chooses ECT must do so competently and without coercion.[3]

Restraints and seclusion should be banned or highly restricted.

Restraints and seclusion also cause a great deal of controversy. Despite the claims of organizations representing hospitals and doctors that these interventions are necessary to maintain safety and order in psychiatric facilities, some facilities are taking active steps to reduce their use. For example, reforms enacted in Pennsylvania's state psychiatric hospitals resulted in a 92 percent reduction in the amount of time that patients spent in seclusion and a 52 percent reduction in the time that patients spent in restraints. According to Charles Curie, the state's former Deputy Secretary for Mental Health and Substance Abuse Services, restraints and seclusion "are not treatment interventions but treatment failures to be used only as a last resort."[4]

Although reducing the use of restraints and seclusion is an admirable goal, many advocates have called for either their abolition or strict limits on their use. In an interview with *USA Today*, Sally Zinman, executive director of the California Network of Mental Health Clients, asked, "Have you ever been in a place where the doors are locked and you don't have the keys?"

THE LETTER OF THE LAW

Texas Law Setting Higher Standards for Informed Consent to ECT than for Other Medical Procedures

Consent to Therapy

(a) The board by rule shall adopt a standard written consent form to be used when electroconvulsive therapy is considered. The board by rule shall also prescribe the information that must be contained in the written supplement required under Subsection (c). In addition to the information required under this section, the form must include the information required by the Texas Medical Disclosure Panel for electroconvulsive therapy. In developing the form, the board shall consider recommendations of the panel. Use of the consent form prescribed by the board in the manner prescribed by this section creates a rebuttable presumption that the disclosure requirements of Sections 6.05 and 6.06, Medical Liability and Insurance Improvement Act of Texas (Article 4590i, Vernon's Texas Civil Statutes), have been met.

(b) The written consent form must clearly and explicitly state:

(1) the nature and purpose of the procedure;

(2) the nature, degree, duration, and probability of the side effects and significant risks of the treatment commonly known by the medical profession, especially noting the possible degree and duration of memory loss, the possibility of permanent irrevocable memory loss, and the possibility of death;

(3) that there is a division of opinion as to the efficacy of the procedure; and

(4) the probable degree and duration of improvement or remission expected with or without the procedure.

(c) Before a patient receives each electroconvulsive treatment, the hospital, facility, or physician administering the therapy shall ensure that:

(1) the patient and the patient's guardian of the person, if any, receives a written copy of the consent form that is in the person's primary language, if possible;

Echoing the sentiments of many advocates, she declared, "Restraint and seclusion are overused. They have killed people." [5]

Gloria Huntley, a 31-year-old Virginia woman, is one of the many people who have died while in restraints. In an

---

    (2) the patient and the patient's guardian of the person, if any, receives a written supplement that contains related information that pertains to the particular patient being treated;

    (3) the contents of the consent form and the written supplement are explained to the patient and the patient's guardian of the person, if any:

        (A) orally, in simple, nontechnical terms in the person's primary language, if possible; or

        (B) through the use of a means reasonably calculated to communicate with a hearing impaired or visually impaired person, if applicable;

    (4) the patient or the patient's guardian of the person, as appropriate, signs a copy of the consent form stating that the person has read the consent form and the written supplement and understands the information included in the documents; and

    (5) the signed copy of the consent form is made a part of the patient's clinical record.

(d) Consent given under this section is not valid unless the person giving the consent understands the information presented and consents voluntarily and without coercion or undue influence.

(e) For a patient 65 years of age or older, before each treatment series begins, the hospital, facility, or physician administering the procedure shall:

    (1) ensure that two physicians have signed an appropriate form that states the procedure is medically necessary;

    (2) make the form described by Subdivision (1) available to the patient or the patient's guardian of the person; and

    (3) inform the patient or the patient's guardian of the person of any known current medical condition that may increase the possibility of injury or death as a result of the treatment.

—Texas Statutes §578.003

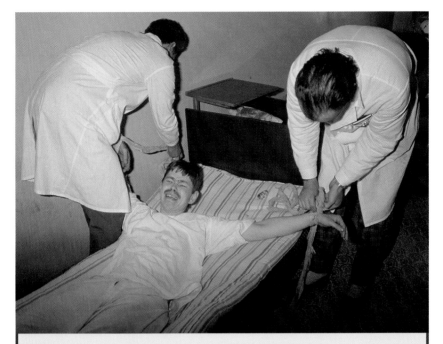

The misuse of restraints in mental hospitals has led to many patient deaths. In 1998, *The Hartford Courant* ran a series of articles chronicling abuses in hospitals nationwide, prompting Congress to enact new legislation limiting the use of restraints.

investigative report, *The Hartford Courant* revealed that she had been "bound to her bed with leather straps for days on end" during a visit by inspectors from the Joint Commission on the Accreditation of Healthcare Organizations (JCAHO), a national association that sets standards for hospitals. In fact, she had been restrained the equivalent of 23 full days in the previous two months. The *Courant* report speculated, "had she been able to move, had she not been pinned down by the wrists and ankles," she might have gotten the attention of the inspectors, who gave the hospital the commission's highest possible score for patients' rights on June 28, 1996.[6] Instead, Huntley died the very next day while still strapped to her bed; this fact was only revealed to investigators after a staff person "blew the whistle" on the hospital, refuting its official claim that Huntley had died in her sleep.

"Unfortunately, the story gets worse," charged Val Marsh, the executive director of the Virginia Alliance for the Mentally Ill, a statewide advocacy group. Prior to her death, Huntley had sought help from a state agency that receives federal funding to protect the rights of people with mental illness. "Huntley was ultimately sent a letter stating (that the agency) had not heard from her in 90 days, assumed that her problems were resolved, and that they were closing her case, with best wishes for her future endeavors. The letter was dated three weeks after she died."[7] A major problem, Marsh asserted, is that the agency designated to protect the rights of psychiatric patients is part of the same state government that runs the psychiatric hospitals in which the patients' rights are violated. Eventually, the state of Virginia settled a lawsuit brought by Huntley's family with the assistance of private attorneys, but by then it was far too late. To many advocates, the tragic events of Gloria Huntley's life and death are proof that the rights of people with mental illness must be guarded much more vigorously.

Involuntary medication should be banned or highly restricted.

Even if a person is involuntarily committed to treatment, the question remains whether the person should be required to take medications. Many mental health advocates, even those who believe that medications can be helpful, oppose "forced drugging." There is considerable support in American jurisprudence for the right to refuse antipsychotic medications. In *Washington v. Harper* (1990), the U.S. Supreme Court recognized this right but held that the Washington prison system could forcibly

Should a government agency, such as the prison system, be allowed to administer medications that affect people's thoughts?

medicate inmate Walter Harper because "the State's interests in prison safety and security" outweighed Harper's right to refuse medications.[8]

However, the outcome of the case rested on Harper's status as a prison inmate, and in his dissent, Justice Stevens made a strong argument that the Fourteenth Amendment creates a "significant liberty interest in avoiding the unwanted administration of antipsychotic drugs." In his view, the right to refuse antipsychotic medication is grounded in the general right to refuse unwanted medical treatment: "Every violation of a person's bodily integrity is an invasion of his or her liberty. . . . Moreover, any such action is degrading if it overrides a competent person's choice to reject a specific form of medical treatment."[9]

Justice Stevens was especially concerned about the involuntary administration of antipsychotic medications due to their powerful effects on the thought process:

> [W]hen the purpose or effect of forced drugging is to alter the will and the mind of the subject, it constitutes a deprivation of liberty in the most literal and fundamental sense. . . . The liberty of citizens to resist the administration of mind altering drugs arises from our Nation's most basic values.[10]

Additionally, maintained Justice Stevens, antipsychotic medications pose a great risk to the individual:

> [T]hese drugs both "alter the chemical balance in a patient's brain" and can cause irreversible and fatal side effects. The prolixin injections that Harper was receiving at the time of his statement exemplify the intrusiveness of psychotropic drugs on a person's body and mind. Prolixin acts "at all levels of the central nervous system as well as on multiple organ systems." It can induce catatonic-like states, alter electroencephalographic tracings, and cause swelling of the brain. Adverse

reactions include drowsiness, excitement, restlessness, bizarre dreams, hypertension, nausea, vomiting, loss of appetite, salivation, dry mouth, perspiration, headache, constipation, blurred vision, impotency, eczema, jaundice, tremors, and muscle spasms. As with all psychotropic drugs, prolixin may cause tardive dyskinesia, an often irreversible syndrome of uncontrollable movements that can prevent a person from exercising basic functions such as driving an automobile, and neuroleptic malignant syndrome, which is 30 percent fatal for those who suffer from it. The risk of side effects increases over time.[11]

> **If a person receives medication against his or her will and then suffers disabling side effects, who should be responsible?**
>
> **Should the patient have the right to sue for money?**
>
> **Should a person's intelligence play a role in determining his or her mental health treatment?**

Many doctors, people with mental illness, and their family members believe that the benefits of medication outweigh the risks. However, many consumer/survivor activists, and organizations such as Support Coalition International, maintain that nobody should be forced to take medication against his or her will. Many people feel that forced drugging is a "chemical straitjacket"—meaning that it is used to control the patient, rather than for treatment purposes.

Families should respect individual treatment choices.

It is not just the mental health system that seeks to exercise more control over people with mental illness. Recall the story of the woman whose family had her committed to a psychiatric hospital after she started dating someone of a different race. The life of Nobel Prize winner John Nash, which was depicted in the book *A Beautiful Mind,* provides an example of the level of control that a family can exercise over a person with mental illness. As the year 1958 came to an end, Nash was one of the most promising young mathematicians in the country. He had developed important theories in the field of "game theory"; theories that would prove useful to the military and to economists and that would eventually help Nash win a Nobel Prize in economics. Before turning 30, he was to be featured in the magazine *Fortune.*

However, in the first two months of 1959, Nash's life began to change drastically. He told colleagues that aliens from space were communicating with him through *The New York Times* and then delivered an incomprehensible speech in front of an audience of hundreds. He began writing strange letters to foreign governments and delivering them to embassies. His colleagues at the Massachusetts Institute of Technology were alarmed. When rumors began to circulate that Nash's wife Alicia planned to have him committed to a psychiatric hospital, the faculty debated "whether, insane or not, anyone had the right to rob a genius like Nash of his freedom,"[12] according to biographer Sylvia Nasar. Nash was committed to a hospital and eventually diagnosed with schizophrenia.

Over the next decade, Nash was hospitalized several times, each time involuntarily, and each time at his family's request. During one hospitalization, Nash was subjected to insulin coma therapy. Five mornings a week, Nash was given a shot of insulin—a hormone that the body produces naturally and that diabetics use to lower their blood sugar—that was so potent that it would cause him to lose consciousness. When he had reached the depths of unconsciousness, a nurse would pump a sugar solution through a tube in Nash's nose, which would increase his blood sugar and allow him to regain consciousness.

> **Does it seem strange that medical techniques that were used in the 1960s are considered barbaric today?**

Although medications are frequently helpful in treating mental illness, patients often need a great deal of support to cope with their illness. The question of how best to treat a given mental illness is a difficult one; the right balance of medications and non-medical programs can be difficult to find.

In addition to being physically draining, the treatment also caused patients, including Nash, to lose large chunks of memory. The medical profession has since completely abandoned insulin coma therapy, and as with the lobotomy, many question why the technique was ever used.

Nash was last hospitalized in 1969, at the request of his sister Martha. She recalled, "I couldn't clean with him in my home. I was here with the children and he's wandering around drinking tea and whistling," and so she had him committed to the hospital. Under the standards of the time, it was not difficult to commit a family member to the hospital: "You didn't have to establish anything drastic,"[13] Martha said. Although most states have much more restrictive commitment standards today, many family advocates are pushing for a return to the broader standards that allowed Nash's family members to have him hospitalized because his behavior was so out of the ordinary.

After being released from the hospital, Nash left his sister's home and spent much of the 1970s and 1980s on the campus of Princeton University, where he had previously studied and taught. Although students were often alarmed by this eccentric and mysterious figure, Nash slowly recovered from schizophrenia without medications or hospitalizations. Eventually, he mended relationships with his wife and family, who had committed him to the hospitals. Perhaps the biggest boost imaginable happened in 1994, when Nash received the Nobel Prize in economics for work that he had done before his illness.

Should journalists report stories that might discourage people with mental illness from taking medications?

Although Nash had not returned to the same level of achievement that he had reached prior to his illness, Nash did begin working in mathematics again. His recovery from schizophrenia has caused a great deal of controversy among the medical and advocacy community, because it challenges the standard medical model of schizophrenia, which holds that it is a chronic disease that requires a lifetime of constant medication and periodic hospitalizations. In an interview with PBS, Nash said: "The drugs I think can be overrated. All of the drugs now continue to have some bad side effects. . . . I am lucky to have come out of mental illness at all, but certainly in the later years I had no drugs."[14]

In the end, Nash credits his own will and determination, rather than medical interventions, for his recovery. "[G]radually I began to intellectually reject some of the delusionally influenced lines of thinking,"[15] he wrote in his Nobel autobiography. For many patients' rights advocates—even those who believe that the use of medication is essential to treatment—Nash's story illustrates the principle that people with mental illness need more control over their own care rather than allowing doctors and family members to determine the course of treatment.

Patients' rights advocates, including many people with mental illness, believe that people need more control over their own mental health treatment. It is fundamentally unfair to treat psychiatric patients differently from other patients, especially when mental health treatments such as electroconvulsive therapy, medications, restraints, and seclusion can be harmful or deadly, advocates say.

Society Cannot Afford to Treat Mental Illness

The costs to society of treating mental illness are staggering. According to the U.S. Surgeon General, the United States spent $69 billion on treating mental illness in 1996—over 7 percent of the nation's annual health care budget. Many people, including politicians, business owners, and ordinary taxpayers, believe that society is simply spending too much money treating mental illnesses, and that something must be done to control costs.

The costs of treating mental illness are too high.

Taxpayers bear a large part of the financial burden of treating people with mental illness. In 1996, over half of the $69 billion spent on treating mental illness came from public funds. Traditionally, the states bore the cost of treating mental illness, usually by building state mental hospitals; today, the federal government provides funding to the states to provide mental health treatment through "community mental health centers." Two important publicly funded insurance programs also spend significant amounts of money on mental health care. Medicaid is an insurance program for low-income people with disabilities; the federal government and the state governments fund Medicaid coverage. Medicare is a federally funded insurance program for older people and for people with disabilities who worked for a significant period of time before becoming disabled.

> **Who should bear the burden of paying for the treatment of people with mental illness—taxpayers, insurance companies, or individuals and their families?**

Some are alarmed at the increases in the cost of treating mental illness. From the years 1986 to 1996, spending on mental health treatment grew at a rate of over 7 percent each year. Significantly, public spending on mental health treatment grew at an even higher rate (over 8 percent), and spending by insurance companies grew by 9 percent. However, the out-of-pocket costs for mental health treatment grew by only 3 percent. Therefore, the taxpayers and insurance companies bore a much larger share of the increased cost of treating mental illness than people with mental illness did.

Why did the costs of treating mental illness increase so drastically? Much of the increases can be tied to increased spending on psychiatric drugs. During the same period, 1986 to 1996, spending on prescription drugs used to treat mental illness increased by almost 10 percent per year, outpacing the growth in mental health expenditures. According to the Surgeon General's report, part of this increase in costs is attributable to increased prescribing of these medications by doctors: between 1985 and 1994, the number of doctor visits during which psychiatric medication was prescribed increased by nearly 40 percent. When advertising prescription drugs to the public became legal in the 1990s, televisions and newspapers suddenly filled with ads, and many patients began to ask doctors for certain medications. *The New England Journal of*

Medicine reported that drug companies' spending on prescription drug advertisements tripled between the years 1996 and 2000.

Much of the increase in psychiatric drug use is tied to the availability of newer antidepressant medications, such as Prozac. Because these newer antidepressants have fewer and less significant side effects than earlier medications, doctors—especially non-psychiatrists—became much more willing to prescribe medications. In fact, family doctors and other non-psychiatrists now prescribe two-thirds of psychiatric medications. This increase in prescriptions has led many people to question whether drugs are being pre-scribed only for people who need them, or whether doctors are prescribing Prozac and other drugs to people who do not need them and would be better off with counseling or even no treatment at all.

If only a doctor can prescribe a drug, should its manufacturer be allowed to advertise it to the public?

Many patient advocates, as well as senior citizens' groups, have also accused drug companies of charging too much for their medications. Although this criticism is not limited to psy-chiatric drugs, many of the drugs used to treat mental illness are quite expensive. In addition to Prozac and other new antide-pressants developed in the 1980s and 1990s, the 1990s also saw the introduction of a number of new antipsychotic medications, which have been used to treat schizophrenia, bipolar disorder, major depression, and other forms of mental illness. These atypical antipsychotic drugs (meaning that they are different from previously available medications), such as Zyprexa, Seroquel, and Risperdal, can be quite costly: a monthly supply for an average patient can cost hundreds of dollars.

Should drug companies be required by law to lower the costs of their products?

Many of the treatments and services for people with mental illness require a lot of time from trained providers, and are therefore very expensive. Many psychotherapists believe that for some people, ongoing sessions are necessary. However, the cost of meeting with a therapist for an hour a week over an extended period of time can be enormous, especially given that therapists frequently charge well over $100 per session. Many people with serious mental illness also receive weekly services from a case manager—a social worker who helps with finding housing, completing daily tasks, complying with treatment, and other activities.

Additionally, many people with mental illness require additional supports because their disability prevents them from working. Many people with mental illness qualify for income support programs and get a monthly check, such as Social Security payments, state welfare subsidies, or Supplemental Security Income (SSI), another federal program. Additionally, many people disabled by mental illness live in government-subsidized housing, receive job training, transportation services, food stamps, and medical and dental care, usually all at taxpayers' expense. These programs all add to the costs of treating mental illness.

Although support services are needed for many people to live in the community rather than being institutionalized in a state hospital, many believe that spending for support services has spiraled out of control. Psychiatrist Sally Satel writes, "The state of Massachusetts shows how far accommodation can go: it actually bought a patient a house and supplied him with attendants twenty-four hours a day."[1] The attendants were needed to allow the man to live in the house because his illness caused him to

> **Should the cost of treating a person in the community determine whether he or she should be kept in a state mental hospital?**

regularly set fires! A mental health official in another county estimated that the $150,000 yearly cost of the housing arrangement was three times the cost of housing the man in the state hospital.

Unnecessary care is partially to blame for rising costs.

In addition to rising costs associated with mental health care, some critics also charge that insurers and taxpayers are footing the bill for a great deal of unnecessary care for people who do not really need it. For example, people who need care might

Demonstrators gather in Boston in November of 2001 to protest cuts to the Massachusetts mental health budget. Too often, the unavailability of services leads to burdens on families, but activists who view mental illness as a physiological disease are working to increase governmental support.

spend more time in the hospital than they really need to. Employers and insurers have charged that some irresponsible professionals provide care based not on what patients need, but on what insurers are willing to pay for. According to a report prepared by the Milbank Memorial Fund, some employers and insurers "claimed that some patients remained hospitalized for as long as insurance picked up most of the bill and then were discharged the day insurance coverage went out."[2]

Many critics of mental health spending also charge that unscrupulous doctors and therapists are more than willing to bill insurance companies for care that people do not need at all. The Milbank report found resentment that people "were seeing psychotherapists month after month because they were dissatisfied with the boss or their spouse or child. Were these really "mental health" problems to be covered by health insurance?"[3]

Sometimes, medical fraud is responsible for increased mental health care costs. A 1999 study by the National Center for Policy Analysis in Dallas reported:

> When Medicare looked for fraud in the community mental health centers last year, it barred 80 of them in nine states from participating in the programs. . . . Medicare administrator Nancy-Ann DeParle contended at the time that 90 percent of the patients had no mental illness serious enough to qualify for special treatment. "You walk into these places and people are playing Bingo and eating lunch," DeParle said.[4]

Should mental health care be rationed, i.e., reserved for those who are the most ill?

What about prevention?

The cost of parity laws requiring equal coverage of mental illness is too high.

Perhaps the one issue regarding mental health financing that has generated the most controversy is insurance parity—requiring insurance plans to provide the same level of coverage for mental illness that they do for physical illness. Many group health insurance plans—such as those provided by a business to its "group" of employees—provide lesser coverage or stricter limits for mental health care than they do for treatment of physical conditions.

The trend toward unequal coverage began in the late 1970s and the 1980s, as employers began to notice that mental health costs were rising much more quickly than other health care costs. To help stem rising insurance prices, insurance plans began to place limits on psychiatric care. Some examples included: higher deductibles, or the amount that an employee had to pay for mental health care before getting reimbursed by the plan; higher copayments, or the amount that an employee had to pay for a psychiatrist visit or psychiatric hospitalization; and annual or lifetime limits on the amount of money that the insurance plan would pay for psychiatric care. Citing federal Bureau of Labor statistics, the Milbank Foundation report revealed a sharp decrease in the number of people who had mental health coverage equal to physical health coverage: in 1993, only 16 percent of people with employer-provided health coverage had coverage for psychiatric hospitalizations that was equal to that for hospitalizations for physical illnesses, down from 58 percent in 1981.[5]

Despite widespread opposition from employers and the insurance industry, Congress passed the Mental Health Parity Act of 1996, which barred group health insurance plans from placing annual or lifetime limits on the amount that the plan

THE LETTER OF THE LAW

The Mental Health Parity Act of 1996

(1) Aggregate lifetime limits
In the case of a group health plan (or health insurance coverage offered in connection with such a plan) that provides both medical and surgical benefits and mental health benefits—

(A) No lifetime limit
If the plan or coverage does not include an aggregate lifetime limit on substantially all medical and surgical benefits, the plan or coverage may not impose any aggregate lifetime limit on mental health benefits.

(B) Lifetime limit
If the plan or coverage includes an aggregate lifetime limit on substantially all medical and surgical benefits (in this paragraph referred to as the "applicable lifetime limit"), the plan or coverage shall either—

(i) apply the applicable lifetime limit both to the medical and surgical benefits to which it otherwise would apply and to mental health benefits and not distinguish in the application of such limit between such medical and surgical benefits and mental health benefits; or

(ii) not include any aggregate lifetime limit on mental health benefits that is less than the applicable lifetime limit.

pays for mental health services that are lower than the limits that the plan pays for other services. However, the effects of the law were not as significant as its sponsors had hoped: although restricted in imposing annual or lifetime dollar limits on psychiatric care, many insurance plans began to limit the number of visits to a psychiatrist that would be covered each year—because there was no dollar limit, this practice was legal under the new law. Additionally, insurance plans could continue to require higher copayments for psychiatric care.

As mental health advocates continued to lobby for a stronger parity law at the federal level, many states enacted their own parity laws. Advocates in other states are also pushing their

(2) Annual limits

In the case of a group health plan (or health insurance coverage offered in connection with such a plan) that provides both medical and surgical benefits and mental health benefits—

(A) No annual limit

If the plan or coverage does not include an annual limit on substantially all medical and surgical benefits, the plan or coverage may not impose any annual limit on mental health benefits.

(B) Annual limit

If the plan or coverage includes an annual limit on substantially all medical and surgical benefits (in this paragraph referred to as the "applicable annual limit"), the plan or coverage shall either—

(I) apply the applicable annual limit both to medical and surgical benefits to which it otherwise would apply and to mental health benefits and not distinguish in the application of such limit between such medical and surgical benefits and mental health benefits; or

(ii) not include any annual limit on mental health benefits that is less than the applicable annual limit.

—42 U.S.C. §300gg-5

legislatures to enact similar laws. However, insurers and many employers think that parity laws are bad for business. Opponents maintain that controlling the cost of mental health care is needed to keep group insurance plans from becoming too expensive. Without limits on mental health coverage, they argue, the rising cost of health insurance will have one of several effects that could end up hurting workers. One result could be that employers simply stop offering health coverage: parity laws require coverage for mental health care equal to that of physical health care, but the laws do not require employers to provide insurance. Another result could be that as insurance plans become more expensive, eligible employees will simply stop paying money out of their paychecks for the coverage offered by their employers. (Many employers pay for part of their employees' health insurance but require employees to pay a monthly fee for the coverage.)

> **Does it make sense for a health insurance plan to pay for some types of medical care but not for others?**

The most pessimistic prediction is that parity will hurt small businesses or drive them out of business. Parity laws have a bigger impact on small businesses than the laws do on large corporations. Many large corporations, which often have thousands of employees, "self insure," or pay for their employee's health care, rather than purchasing group insurance plans; self-insurance is not covered by parity laws because it is regulated by the federal Employee Retirement Income Security Act (ERISA). Therefore, because parity would raise health insurance costs for small businesses that buy group insurance but not for large corporations that do not, it would make it more difficult for small businesses to compete with large corporations. Also, because people want health coverage, small businesses that cannot afford to offer expensive health insurance plans will not be able to recruit qualified employees.

It is difficult to determine exactly how much parity laws increase the cost of health plans. In most states that have enacted parity laws, insurers have sought to control mental health costs through managed care techniques, such as requiring pre-approval for psychiatric visits and only approving a few therapy sessions at a time. Although in those states, insurance costs have not risen dramatically, opponents of parity argue that the savings associated with managed care's cost-saving techniques have simply cancelled out the increased costs of parity. The insurance industry also has an answer to parity supporters' claims that implementing parity would actually lower insurance costs because coverage allows people to see a mental health professional before their problems become severe. As an executive representing health plans in Wisconsin told *The Milwaukee Business Journal*, "If that is indeed true, then businesses don't need a law to compel them to find cost savings."[6]

Should people or businesses be required to do things that benefit them?

Who should decide what will benefit whom?

Should there be exceptions?

Opponents of mental health spending believe that costs have gotten out of control. Unlimited spending, they say, encourages people to seek treatment that they do not need, and encourages doctors to provide that treatment. Newer medications and other treatments are too expensive, and therefore many oppose parity laws that require insurance policies to cover mental illness at the same level as physical illness.

Society Cannot Afford *Not* to Treat Mental Illness

M ental health advocates reject the argument that mental health care is too expensive for society to afford. Fairness requires society to provide healthcare to people who need it, regardless of their type of illness. People with mental illness can recover and regain some or all of their lost productivity, but only if society provides the supports that they need to succeed.

The costs of treating mental illness are rising more slowly than the costs of health care.

When critics of mental health spending point to rising costs, mental health advocates respond that costs for *all* forms of health care have been going up. According to the U.S. Surgeon General's report, although mental health spending increased by more than 7 percent per year between 1986 and 1996, overall health spending increased by more than 8 percent. Therefore, mental health costs have been actually decreasing as a percentage of the nation's health care budget.

Additionally, when viewed through the lens of rising health care costs, states are spending much less on mental health care than they used to. According to a report by the Bazelon Center for

Is it unfair to criticize increases in mental health spending when spending in other areas is also increasing, or is it fair to criticize greater spending?

Mental Health Law, the states are spending less—taking into account inflation (rising prices) and population growth—on mental health care in 1997 than they did in 1955, which was the year during which psychiatric hospitalizations were the highest. The report also revealed the following:

> State appropriations for mental health have also experienced much lower increases than total state spending and spending for corrections. During the 1990s, states' expenditures for mental health services grew 33 percent, while total state spending grew 56 percent and spending on corrections, 68 percent. As a result, the share of state spending devoted to mental health is dropping—by 15 percent from 1990 to 1997.[1]

More significant, many say, than the costs of mental health treatment are the indirect costs of unabated mental illness, such as decreased productivity in the workplace. For example, according to the Surgeon General's report, mental illness imposed greater indirect costs on society than cancer did: mental illness caused a $79 billion loss to the U.S. economy in 1990; compare that figure to the $69 billion spent on treating mental illness in 1996. The report measured decreased productivity caused by missed work, early deaths, incarceration, and family care.

Many feel that even the large figure contained in the

report is too conservative. The report itself acknowledged: "These indirect cost estimates are conservative because they do not capture some measure of the pain, suffering, disruption, and reduced productivity that are not reflected in earnings."[2] With estimates that people with mental illness make up between 5 and 20 percent of the nation's jail and prison population, many feel that the correctional system is spending money incarcerating people who simply needed mental health treatment. However, because treatment is so frequently unavailable, many people with mental illness spend time in jail for "nuisance crimes," such as vagrancy or trespassing.

Is it wise to spend taxpayers' money to improve the productivity of private citizens?

It is impossible to determine the extent to which increased spending will reduce indirect costs. However, it is clear that people who receive no treatment, or substandard treatment, for mental illness impose great indirect costs upon society. U.S. Representative Patrick Kennedy (D-RI) testified before a Congressional subcommittee: "An inability to receive proper medical care turns potential wage earners and taxpayers into welfare recipients. Those who remain in the workforce with untreated mental illnesses are twice as likely as their colleagues to miss work." To support his contentions, he read a letter from a Kentucky woman:

In 1998 I was hospitalized 3 times for depression with suicidal intent. Each hospitalization was terminated, not because my doctor felt I was ready to leave, but because my insurance company refused to pay for further treatment. When I left the hospital the last time, I was still severely depressed. I was not healthy enough to return to my teaching career of 24 years. Since I had exhausted all my leave days, I was forced to resign my job and go on disability retirement.[3]

Sen. Pete Domenici (R-NM, at left, shown with President George W. Bush) has been a strong supporter of federal parity laws, which would end insurance discrimination against mental health treatment.

Studies suggest that employees with mental illness are many times more likely to miss work than their coworkers are. However, the Americans with Disabilities Act, a federal law, prohibits workplace discrimination against people with mental illnesses and requires employers to make "reasonable accommodations" for people's disabilities.

Is it fair to ask an employer to accommodate someone who misses a lot of work due to illness?

How often should a person be allowed to miss work before it is no longer "reasonable"?

The result of higher costs is better care.

Mental health advocates believe that much of the increases in spending on mental health care have resulted in positive improvements in Americans' overall health. Take the example of the increase in the number of people diagnosed with and treated for depression since the introduction of newer anti-depressants—such as Prozac—with fewer side effects. Critics of mental health spending argue that this increase in diag-noses is due to an increase in treatment of the "worried well," who do not really need treatment. While mental health advocates acknowledge that some of the costs of treating mental illness can be attributed to people seeking care that they do not really need, or to doctors providing care to people who do not really need it, the answer, they say, is greater over-sight of care rather than a flat denial or lesser coverage of mental health services.

Mental health advocates say that the lesser side effects of Prozac and similar drugs mean family doctors can prescribe them; therefore, people who might have been embarrassed or ashamed to seek psychiatric help are getting the help they need from the family doctors whom they trust. Many mental health advocates believe that it is good that more people are seeking mental health services. To some, it indicates a break-ing down of the "stigma" of mental illness. As defined by the Center for Mental Health Services, a federal agency, stigma

> . . . is not just the use of the wrong word or action. Stigma is about disrespect. It is the use of negative labels to identify a person living with mental illness. Stigma is a barrier and discourages individuals and their families from getting the help they need due to the fear of being discriminated against. An estimated 50 million Americans experience a mental disorder in any given year and only one-fourth of them actually receive mental health and other services.[4]

Through active anti-stigma campaigns, mental health advocates hope to encourage more people to seek treatment for mental illness. Mental health advocates have different approaches to reducing stigma. Some believe that emphasizing the biological basis of mental illness helps to reduce the stigma of mental illness, which many people continue to regard as a character flaw. Others believe that emphasizing the availability of effective treatment will encourage people to seek help.

> **How can the knowledge that mental illness is often based in physiology change the public perception of people with mental illness?**

In an era of managed care, many people with mental illness are finding that their insurance policies will not cover regular psychotherapy sessions. Many psychotherapists recommend weekly hour-long counseling sessions, but insurance companies often will only pay for monthly 15-minute appointments to discuss the patients' medications and side effects, rather than a person's emotional concerns.

Although providing psychotherapy can be expensive, many advocates argue that it can be worth the cost because psychotherapy is so important in treating depression and other mental illnesses, thus eliminating some of the indirect costs of mental illness. Psychotherapy in combination with medications is much more effective than medications alone. One study revealed, "[T]reatment with a combination of [an antidepressant] and psychotherapy had significant advantages over treatment with [an antidepressant] or psychotherapy alone."[5] The study found positive results in 85 percent of patients receiving both the antidepressant and psychotherapy, compared to just over half of the patients receiving only one or the other.

Another reason why mental health spending benefits society is that the newer, more expensive antipsychotic medications help people live and work in the community, thus reducing their reliance on expensive hospitalizations and public support. Advocates criticize managed care policies that restrict access to atypical antipsychotic drugs, or require patients to "fail first" on the older medications.

Late consumer advocate Ken Steele's experience shows that people who had been disabled and tormented for years were able to lead successful lives for the first time after beginning to take atypical antipsychotic medications. Over 30 years, Steele heard voices that made "demeaning and horrid statements" to him, warned him that people were trying to harm him, and ordering him to kill himself. During this time, he was hospitalized for extended periods of time, and at other times lived in halfway houses, group homes, or on the streets; he made numerous suicide attempts at the command of the voices in his head. He tried a dozen different medications but suffered from side effects, and the voices continued.

> **Is it acceptable to require a person to take a certain medication, despite side effects or a low rate of efficacy, if that medication is far less expensive than something more effective?**

However, in 1993, Steele was prescribed an atypical antipsychotic medication. Although the voices ordered him not to take the medication, he eventually began taking the medication regularly. "Then, in early 1995, the voices stopped completely."[6] Although it took some time to adjust to living without the voices, Steele took advantage of his wellness to help other people with mental illness. He helped to register thousands of people with mental illness to vote—although eligible to vote, many people with mental illness do not know about this right or are actively discouraged from voting. He also began a newspaper, *New York City Voices*, which is written and published completely by people with mental illness. Despite Steele's death in October 2000, his work lives on and has inspired a nationwide voter registration project based on the one in New York.

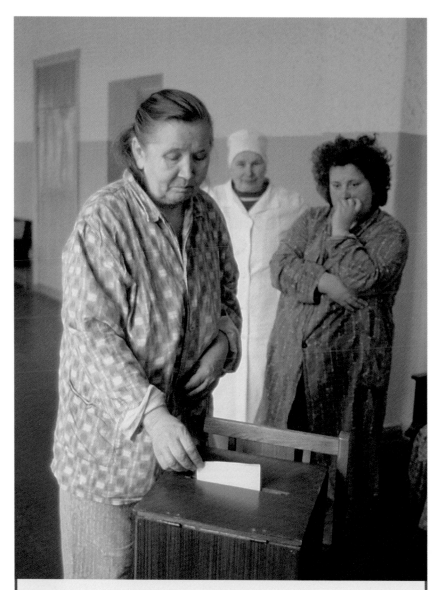

The right to vote is among the most fundamental rights of a U.S. citizen, but for many years people with mental illness have been denied this right. Thanks to the work of advocates like the late Ken Steele, more people with mental illness are exercising their right to vote.

Laws requiring equal coverage for mental illness are necessary.

Mental health advocates believe that it is fundamentally unfair to deny people coverage for mental health care that is equal to that for other types of health care. As Congressman Patrick Kennedy (D-RI) testified before Congress:

> Lives are lost every day because teenagers, seniors, and others can't get the treatment they need. For every two homicides in this nation, there are three suicides, and in 90 percent of those cases, the victim had a diagnosable mental disorder. . . .
>
> I am confident that . . . nobody in this Congress (would condone) rationing health care for cancer or asthma. Like mental illnesses these are potentially fatal, frequently treatable, chronic diseases. Unlike cancer and asthma patients, however, most Americans suffering from mental illnesses find that their health plans hinder access to necessary medical treatment.
>
> If we would not tell asthma or cancer patients that their coverage is too expensive, why would we say that to the mentally ill?
>
> Essentially, we are asking the mentally ill to sacrifice potentially life-saving treatment in order to keep health care costs down for everybody else. The unfairness of that request is manifest.[7]

Should a person who has been institutionalized in a mental hospital have the right to vote?

What about a person who is in a hospital for a chronic physical illness?

Some parity advocates are especially upset that insurance plans exclude treatment for mental illness, which scientists continue to show have a physiological basis, just like any other illness. Another contradiction is that some plans provide lesser coverage for mental illnesses, which are not thought to be preventable. By contrast, preventable physical conditions that can be linked to behavior are covered fully by insurance plans: a heavy smoker's treatment for lung cancer would be covered fully; an alcoholic's treatment for cirrhosis of the liver would be covered fully; and a sexually promiscuous person's treatment for a sexually transmitted disease would be covered fully. However, a person who develops depression or schizophrenia—even though he or she has never done anything known to cause the illness— would receive lesser coverage under a health plan.

Advocates of parity laws also argue that the costs of

THE LETTER OF THE LAW

Excerpt from Vermont's Parity Law

(b) A health insurance plan shall provide coverage for treatment of a mental health condition and shall not establish any rate, term or condition that places a greater financial burden on an insured for access to treatment for a mental health condition than for access to treatment for a physical health condition. Any deductible or out-of-pocket limits required under a health insurance plan shall be comprehensive for coverage of both mental health and physical health conditions.

(c) A health insurance plan that does not otherwise provide for management of care under the plan, or that does not provide for the same degree of management of care for all health conditions, may provide coverage for treatment of mental health conditions through a managed care organization provided that the managed care organization is in compliance with the rules adopted by the commissioner that assure that the system for delivery of treatment for mental health conditions does not diminish or negate the purpose of this section. The rules adopted by the commissioner shall assure that timely and appropriate access to care is available; that the quantity, location and specialty distribution of health care providers is adequate and that administrative or clinical protocols do not serve to reduce access to medically necessary treatment for any insured.

—8 Vermont Stat. Ann., §4089b

implementing parity are minimal. The Surgeon General's report concluded:

> Until recently, efforts to achieve parity in insurance coverage for the treatment of mental disorders were hampered by limited information on the effects of such mandates. This led to wide variations in estimates of the costs of implementing such laws. For example, past estimates of the increase in premium costs of full parity in proposed federal legislation have ranged from 3 percent to more than 10 percent. . . .
>
> Case studies of five states that had a parity law for at least a year revealed a small effect on premiums—at most a change of a few percent, plus or minus. . . . Separate studies of laws in Texas, Maryland, and North Carolina have shown that costs actually declined after parity was introduced where legislation coincided with the introduction of managed care. In general, the number of users increased, with lower average expenditures per user.[8]

In fact, some advocates argue, parity actually saves businesses money by treating mental illnesses that would otherwise result in lost workdays and diminished productivity. Additionally, some advocates believe that parity removes barriers to seeking treatment, thus encouraging workers to seek treatment for depression and other conditions sooner than they would if they had to pay high out-of-pocket costs. By getting treatment early, the workers might be able to prevent the condition from becoming more serious, which would result in lost work, expensive hospitalizations, and perhaps even disability payments.

Mental health advocates believe that society should pay for mental health treatment, both as a matter of fairness and compassion, and because the societal effects of untreated mental

illness—such as lost productivity and homelessness—
are greater than the costs of treating mental illness. While
treatment might be expensive, advocates say, it helps people
become productive members of society. Insurance parity laws
requiring equal coverage of mental illness and physical illness
are desperately needed, they maintain, and do not increase
insurance costs significantly.

The Future of Mental Health Rights

L ike cancer, AIDS, and other conditions that impose tremendous costs on society, mental illness will remain a subject of controversy. As with other medical conditions, mental health advocates will continue to push for more research and better access to treatment for the poor and minorities. However, mental illness is different from other conditions in that scientists know so little about what causes mental illness or how to prevent it. And the public continues to have many misperceptions about mental illness despite widespread public education campaigns.

The question of violence will probably remain the most controversial issue regarding mental illness. Although studies have shown that the vast majority of people with mental illness are no more dangerous than their neighbors, high profile events such as the "subway pushers" in New York City will continue to shape public opinion, and politicians will continue to push for laws that make it easier to involuntarily commit a person with mental illness to treatment. Many mental health advocates argue that the answer to the societal problems caused by mental illness is neither involuntary treatment nor jailing people with mental illness for nuisance crimes, such as littering or trespassing. Rather, the solution is to provide more comprehensive services to people in the community, including housing, newer medications, psychotherapy, job training, and other supports.

> **Do people with mental illness pose a greater threat to the community than others do?**
>
> **What would be a reliable test of dangerousness?**

Are Mental Health Courts an Answer?

As states have closed their psychiatric hospitals, the states have not provided an equivalent level of services in the community. As a result, many jails and prisons have become the largest "mental health providers" in their jurisdictions. To deal with the problem of the "criminalization" of mental illness, many jurisdictions have started separate "mental health courts" to hear cases involving people with mental illness who are charged with non-violent crimes. Rather than sentencing defendants to prison, the mental health courts mandate a treatment program, which can include medication, case management, and hospitalization or outpatient treatment.

Mental health advocates differ widely in their opinions about mental health courts. Some favor the courts as a means of linking people with needed mental health services. Opponents of involuntary treatment, on the other hand, see mental health courts as a danger. Others are concerned that mental health courts are a "quick fix" for a lack of voluntary, community-based services.

Proponents of mental health courts argue that people with mental illness who commit non-violent crimes should not be sent to jails or prisons because correctional facilities cannot adequately serve their mental health needs. Correctional facilities are understaffed and do not provide access to newer medications. Also, correctional facilities often respond to manic or psychotic behavior with punitive measures such as seclusion or restraint—measures that cause further trauma. However, some opponents feel that the alternative provided by mental health courts—treatment in a community or hospital setting—is yet another avenue for forced treatment.

Should people with mental illness be kept out of correctional facilities that cannot meet their needs? What are their needs?

Can the same be argued of juvenile offenders?

How far must such facilities go to meet the individual needs of inmates?

Another benefit of mental health courts, supporters argue, is that people avoid convictions for relatively minor crimes. On the other hand, mental health courts allow for people with mental illness who commit nuisance crimes to be forced into a mandatory treatment regimen, whereas people without a psychiatric diagnosis would not be prosecuted for such minor crimes. Thus, opponents argue, mental health courts provide a means to use minor crimes as an excuse for involuntary treatment.

Cost is at the center of any public policy debate, and proponents argue that mental health courts are cost-effective because they divert people from expensive periods of incarceration. However, many advocates are concerned that, just as money from state hospitals usually did not follow people into the community, the monetary savings from mental health courts will not be used to improve community-based mental health programs.

Will Society Embrace Recovery?

Another recent trend in mental health policy is trying to determine what the system can do to support the "recovery model" of mental illness. Simply stated, this is the view that people can recover from mental illness to regain their roles in life: friend, parent, worker, or church member, for example. This is much different from traditional views of mental illness as a permanent disability that can be treated with medication but can never be cured.

Definitions of recovery vary. Some say that recovery means a complete absence of symptoms without any use of medication. Others believe that recovery also includes the complete control of symptoms through the use of medications and other treatments. The broadest definition of recovery

What is "recovery" in the context of mental illness?

includes people who still experience symptoms, such as hearing voices, but have learned ways to live with these symptoms so that they are able to lead meaningful lives.

However recovery is defined, hard work is required for a mental health system to embrace the concept. Most important is changing the attitudes of the people who work within the system: many mental health professionals have for years thought of people with mental illness as having incurable conditions that would make them forever dependent on public support. But like patients who recover from spinal cord injuries and are either able to walk again or live full lives despite an ongoing physical disability, more and more people with mental illness are—like Nobel Prize winner John Nash—recovering from even the most serious mental illnesses.

Mental health reform is an ongoing process. And it is certainly not an easy one. People who think of themselves as advocates for people with mental illness can have many different opinions on a single issue. Advocates might disagree on such key issues as involuntary treatment, medications, electroconvulsive therapy, seclusion, and restraint. Everyone would like to see a nation in which there are fewer stories like Andrew Goldstein's and more like that of John Nash, but questions remain: What is the best way of getting to that point? And who will pay for it?

Defining Mental Illness

1 Michael Winerip, "Bedlam on the Streets," *New York Times Sunday Magazine*, May 23, 1999.

2 Michael Winerip, "Bedlam on the Streets," *New York Times Sunday Magazine*, May 23, 1999.

3 National Institute of Mental Health, *Schizophrenia*, pub. no. 00–3517, 1–2.

4 National Institute of Mental Health, *Schizophrenia*, pub. no. 00–3517, 5.

5 National Institute of Mental Health, *Schizophrenia*, pub. no. 00–3517, 5.

Point: Inpatient and Outpatient Commitment Laws Are Not Strong Enough

1 Treatment Advocacy Center, *Model Law for Assisted Treatment*, 3.

2 Treatment Advocacy Center, press release dated 13 June 2000.

3 Laura Parker, "Families Lobby to Force Care," *USA Today*, 12 February 2001.

4 Philip T. Ninan and Rosalind Mance, "Schizophrenia and Other Psychotic Disorders," in *Clinical Psychiatry for Medical Students*, ed. Alan Stoudemire (Philadelphia: J.B. Lippincott, 1994).

5 Treatment Advocacy Center, *Model Law for Assisted Treatment*, vii.

6 Treatment Advocacy Center, *Model Law for Assisted Treatment*, viii.

7 William Kanapaux, "Outpatient Commitment Builds Momentum," *Behavioral Healthcare Tomorrow* (October 1999), 12.

8 U.S. Surgeon General, *Mental Health: A Report of the Surgeon General* (1999), 291–292.

9 Governor George E. Pataki, press release dated 19 May 1999.

Counterpoint: Inpatient and Outpatient Commitment Laws Violate Rights

1 New York State Consolidated Laws, Mental Hygiene, §9.60.

2 *O'Connor v. Donaldson*, 422 U.S. 563, 575 (1975).

3 *Kansas v. Crane*, Slip op. no. 00957 (January 22, 2002).

4 Bruce J. Winick, "The Civil Commitment Hearing: Applying the Law Therapeutically," in *The Evolution of Mental Health Law*, ed. Lynda E. Frost and Richard J. Bonnie (Washington, D.C.: American Psychological Association, 2001), 293.

5 Joseph F. Duffy, "New York Passes Bill Creating Involuntary Outpatient Pilot Program for the Mentally Ill," *Psychiatric Times* XI, no. 10 (October 1994), 5.

6 John Q. La Fond and Mary L. Durham, *Back to the Asylum* (New York: Oxford University Press, 1992), 112.

7 H. Steadman, E. Mulvey, J. Monahan, et al., "Violence by People Discharged from Acute Psychiatric Inpatient Facilities and by Others in the Same Neighborhoods." *Archives of General Psychiatry*, 55 (1998), 393. Cited at www.macarthur.virginia.edu/violence.html.

8 *Cruzan v. Director, MDH*, 497 U.S. 261, 309 (1990) (Brennan, J., dissenting).

9 Elaine Sutton Mbionwu, "Involuntary Outpatient Commitment: If It Isn't Voluntary . . . Maybe It Isn't Treatment," *Protection & Advocacy Systems News* 4, no. 5 (Winter 1999).

10 RAND Corporation, *Does Involuntary Outpatient Commitment Work: Research Brief 4537* (Santa Monica, Calif.: RAND Distribution Services, 2000).

11 International Association of Psychosocial Rehabilitation Services, "IAPSRS Statement on Involuntary Outpatient Commitment," *PSR Connection* (March 2000), 3.

Point: Doctors, Hospitals, and Family Members Need More Control Over the Treatment of People with Mental Illness

1 John Q. La Fond and Mary L. Durham, *Back to the Asylum* (New York: Oxford University Press, 1992), 113.

2 Laura Parker, "Families Lobby to Force Care," *USA Today*, 12 February 2001.

3 American Psychiatric Association, *Let's Talk: Facts About Electroconvulsive Therapy (ECT)*, Washington, DC: American Psychiatric Association, 1996.

4 American Psychiatric Association, *Let's Talk: Facts About Electroconvulsive Therapy (ECT)*, Washington, DC: American Psychiatric Association, 1996.

5 Statement of the American Psychiatric Association to the Senate Labor–HHS Appropriations Subcommittee, April 13, 1999.

6 Statement of the American Psychiatric Association to the Senate Labor–HHS Appropriations Subcommittee, April 13, 1999.

7 42 U.S.C. §290ii.

8 American Psychiatric Association, *Talking Points on Seclusion and Restraint*, available at *www.psych.org*.

9 Sally Satel, *PC, M.D.: How Political Correctness Is Corrupting Medicine* (New York: Basic Books, 2000), 56.

10 Sally Satel, *PC, M.D.: How Political Correctness Is Corrupting Medicine* (New York: Basic Books, 2000), 75.

11 Laura Parker, "Families Lobby to Force Care," *USA Today*, 12 February 2001.

12 Laura Parker, "Families Lobby to Force Care," *USA Today*, 12 February 2001.

13 Jerry Delk, "How I Became an Advocate for the Mentally Ill," *www.collinsville-baptistchurch.com/delk1.htm*.

Counterpoint: People with Mental Illness Need More Control Over Their Own Treatment

1 *Schloendorff v. Society of New York Hospital*, 211 N.Y. 125, 129–30 (1914).

2 Liz Spikol, "Shocked and Appalled," *Philadelphia Weekly*, 7 February 2001.

3 National Mental Health Association, "Position Statement on Electro-convulsive Therapy," 11 June 2000.

4 NAMI Pennsylvania, "Pennsylvania Leads the Country in Reducing the Use of Seclusion and Restraints," *The Alliance*, Fall 1999, 8.

5 Laura Parker, "Families Lobby to Force Care," *USA Today*, 12 February 2001.

6 Eric M. Weiss and Dave Altimari, "Patients Suffer in a System Without Oversight," *Hartford Courant*, 13 October 1998.

7 Val Marsh, "Virginia's Failure to Protect and Advocate," *The Network* 13, no. 2 (July 1997).

8 *Washington v. Harper*, 494 U.S. 210, 223 (1990).

9 *Washington v. Harper*, 494 U.S. 210, 237 (1990).

10 *Washington v. Harper*, 494 U.S. 210, 237–38 (1990).

11 *Washington v. Harper*, 494 U.S. 210, 239–40 (1990).

12 Sylvia Nasar, *A Beautiful Mind: The Life of Mathematical Genius and Nobel Laureate John Nash* (New York: Simon & Schuster, 1998), 253.

13 Sylvia Nasar, *A Beautiful Mind: The Life of Mathematical Genius and Nobel Laureate John Nash* (New York: Simon & Schuster, 1998), 331.

14 Featured in "A Brilliant Madness" on *www.pbs.org*.

15 John F. Nash, Jr., "Autobiography," featured on *www.nobel.se*.

Point: Society Cannot Afford to Treat Mental Illness

1 Sally Satel, *PC, M.D.: How Political Correctness Is Corrupting Medicine* (New York: Basic Books, 2000), 58.

2 Alan L. Otten, *Mental Health Parity: What Can It Accomplish in a Market Dominated by Managed Care?* (New York: Milbank Foundation, 1998).

3 Alan L. Otten, *Mental Health Parity: What Can It Accomplish in a Market Dominated by Managed Care?* (New York: Milbank Foundation, 1998).

4 Merrill Matthews Jr., *Brief Analysis 297, Do We Need Mental Health Parity?* (Dallas: National Center for Policy Analysis, 1997).

5 Alan L. Otten, *Mental Health Parity: What Can It Accomplish in a Market Dominated by Managed Care?* (New York: Milbank Foundation, 1998).

6 Julie Sneider, "Business Groups Oppose Mental Health Coverage Plan," *Milwaukee Business Journal,* 25 January 2002.

Counterpoint: Society Cannot Afford *Not* to Treat Mental Illness

1 Robert Bernstein and Chris Koyanagi, *Disintegrating Systems: The State of States' Public Mental Health Systems* (Washington, D.C.: Bazelon Center for Mental Health Law, 2001), 15.

2 U.S. Surgeon General, *Mental Health: A Report of the Surgeon General* (1999), 411.

3 Testimony of the Honorable Patrick J. Kennedy, U.S. House of Representatives, 13 March 2002.

4 See *www.mentalhealth.org/stigma.*

5 Martin B. Keller et al., "A Comparison of Nefazodone, the Cognitive Behavioral-Analysis System of Psychotherapy, and Their Combination for the Treatment of Chronic Depression," *New England Journal of Medicine* 342 (18 May 2000): 1462–1470.

6 Ken Steele, "One Patient's Journey to Mental Wellness," *New York City Voices,* November/December 1997.

7 Testimony of the Honorable Patrick J. Kennedy, U.S. House of Representatives, 13 March 2002.

8 U.S. Surgeon General, *Mental Health: A Report of the Surgeon General* (1999), 411.

98

American Psychiatric Association. *Let's Talk: Facts About Electroconvulsive Therapy (ECT)*. American Psychiatric Association, 1996.

Bernstein, Robert and Chris Koyanagi. *Disintegrating Systems: The State of States' Public Mental Health Systems*. Bazelon Center for Mental Health Law, 2001.

La Fond, John Q. and Mary L. Durham. *Back to the Asylum*. Oxford University Press, 1992.

Nasar, Sylvia. *A Beautiful Mind: The Life of Mathematical Genius and Nobel Laureate John Nash*. Simon & Schuster, 1998.

National Institute of Mental Health. *Schizophrenia*. Pub. no. 00-3517.

Ninan, Philip T. and Rosalind Mance. "Schizophrenia and Other Psychotic Disorders." In *Clinical Psychiatry for Medical Students*, ed. Alan Stoudemire. J.B. Lippincott, 1994.

Otten, Alan L. *Mental Health Parity: What Can It Accomplish in a Market Dominated by Managed Care?* Milbank Foundation, 1998.

RAND Corporation. *Does Involuntary Outpatient Commitment Work?: Research Brief 4537*. RAND Distribution Services, 2000.

Satel, Sally. *PC, M.D.: How Political Correctness Is Corrupting Medicine*. Basic Books, 2000.

Treatment Advocacy Center. *Model Law for Assisted Treatment*. Available at *www.psychlaws.org*.

U.S. Surgeon General. *Mental Health: A Report of the Surgeon General*. U.S. Surgeon General, 1999.

Winick, Bruce J. "The Civil Commitment Hearing: Applying the Law Therapeutically." In *The Evolution of Mental Health Law*, eds. Lynda E. Frost and Richard J. Bonnie. American Psychological Association, 2001.

The Bazelon Center for Mental Health Law

www.bazelon.org
Advocacy center with frequent updates concerning legislation and public policy; vast resources on a number of topics related to mental health.

Information About Electroconvulsive Therapy

www.ect.org
A website critical of electroconvulsive therapy (ECT), expressing the views of activists who have undergone the procedure.

The International Association of Psychosocial Rehabilitation Services

www.iapsrs.org

An international organization dedicated to providing rehabilitation services to people with mental illness; information on current issues in treatment and community support.

The Joint Commission on Accreditation of Healthcare Organizations

www.jcaho.org

Independent organization that inspects and rates hospitals and other healthcare organizations; provides quality listings.

U.S. Department of Health and Human Services: Substance Abuse and Mental Health Services Administration: Center for Mental Health Services

www.mentalhealth.org

Federal agency that provides support to local and state mental health systems and deals with the societal aspects of mental illness. Fine source of information by state, including statistics and program listings.

National Mental Health Consumers' Self-Help Clearinghouse

www.mhselfhelp.org

Much information on referral and on advocacy, especially self-advocacy; the "Political Stuff" section provides a solid background on managed care.

The National Alliance for the Mentally Ill

www.nami.org

A national organization that has traditionally represented family members of people with mental illness; provides information on biological basis of mental illness and on current advocacy issues.

The National Center for Policy Analysis

www.ncpa.org

Reviews national policy in many subdomains; aims to find private-sector modes of solving problems of public policy. Especially worth a visit is the site's extensive "Both Sides" area.

New York City Voices: A Consumer Journal for Mental Health Advocacy

www.newyorkcityvoices.org

A NYC-based journal that welcomes submissions on all aspects of mental health; offers many accounts of personal experience and many opinions by practitioners in the field.

The National Institute of Mental Health (NIMH)

www.nimh.nih.gov

A branch of the federal National Institutes of Health that offers a wealth of resources for researchers and the public, including updates on clinical trials that are currently in progress.

The National Mental Health Association

www.nmha.org
A national non-profit organization created to improve mental health across
the board. A source of current information on surveys, press releases, and new
publications. Contains an extensive section on advocacy.

The National Association of Protection and Advocacy Systems (NAPAS)

www.protectionandadvocacy.com
Organization representing each state's federally funded "protection and advocacy"
agency, which protects the rights of people with disabilities. Provides information
about legal issues involving people with disabilities.

The American Psychiatric Association

www.psych.org
National organization representing psychiatrists. Provides medical information
written for the general public.

The Treatment Advocacy Center

www.psychlaws.org
A one-sided site that includes an "episodes database" detailing "preventable
tragedies"; excellent source of abstracts of articles appearing in the major
medical journals; gives treatment laws by state.

The RAND Corporation

www.rand.org
A nonprofit organization founded by the U.S. military just after World War II;
devoted to research and development and analysis of applications of new
information to debates on public policy. Works in many subdomains.

Sally Satel, M.D.

www.sallysatelmd.com
Homepage of noted and controversial psychiatrist and author Sally Satel, whose
work focuses on the connection between politics and health care; argues that
myths and ideas of social justice are compromising patient care.

Office of the Surgeon General of the United States

www.surgeongeneral.gov
The Surgeon General heads the U.S. Public Health Services. Site publishes
in-depth reports on many aspects of public health, including mental health.

Legislation and Case Law

Schloendorff v. Society of New York Hospital, 211 N.Y. 125, 129–130 (1914)
Affirmed in 1914 that to impose medical care on an unwilling patient violated
that patient's rights.

O'Connor v. Donaldson, 422 U.S. 563 (1975)
Affirmed that a finding of "mental illness" alone—i.e., without proof of threat—
is not sufficient to justify commitment by the state.

Washington v. Harper, 494 U.S. 210, 223 (1990)
Considering forced medication with antipsychotic drugs, affirmed the patient's
general right to deny medication but allowed an exception in the interest of
prison security.

Cruzan v. Director, MDH, 497 U.S. 261, 309 (1990)
Affirmed a patient's right to refuse medical treatment.

The Mental Health Parity Act of 1996
Attempted to broaden insurance coverage for people with mental illness, to bring
this coverage more into alignment with coverage for physical illness, by reducing
limitations on services of certain kinds.

"Kendra's Law," New York State Consolidated Laws, Mental Hygiene,
§9.60 (1999)
Made it easier either to institutionalize people with mental illness or to compel
them to follow a program of medication, whether "dangerousness" has been
shown or not.

Kansas v. Crane, Slip op. no. 00957 (January 22, 2002)
Clarified the standards for civil commitment: (1) that the commitment be "by
the book," i.e., by established rules with proper evidence; (2) that the person be
shown to be dangerous to herself or to others; and (3) that the person be shown
to suffer from "mental illness or mental abnormality."

Concepts and Standards

gravely disabled

danger to self and others

outpatient commitment

informed consent

guardian of the person

Beginning Legal Research

The goal of POINT/COUNTERPOINT is not only to provide the reader with an introduction to a controversial issue affecting society, but also to encourage the reader to explore the issue more fully. This appendix, then, is meant to serve as a guide to the reader in researching the current state of the law as well as exploring some of the public-policy arguments as to why existing laws should be changed or new laws are needed.

Like many types of research, legal research has become much faster and more accessible with the invention of the Internet. This appendix discusses some of the best starting points, but of course "surfing the Net" will uncover endless additional sources of information—some more reliable than others. Some important sources of law are not yet available on the Internet, but these can generally be found at the larger public and university libraries. Librarians usually are happy to point patrons in the right direction.

The most important source of law in the United States is the Constitution. Originally enacted in 1787, the Constitution outlines the structure of our federal government and sets limits on the types of laws that the federal government and state governments can pass. Through the centuries, a number of amendments have been added to or changed in the Constitution, most notably the first ten amendments, known collectively as the Bill of Rights, which guarantee important civil liberties. Each state also has its own constitution, many of which are similar to the U.S. Constitution. It is important to be familiar with the U.S. Constitution because so many of our laws are affected by its requirements. State constitutions often provide protections of individual rights that are even stronger than those set forth in the U.S. Constitution.

Within the guidelines of the U.S. Constitution, Congress—both the House of Representatives and the Senate—passes bills that are either vetoed or signed into law by the President. After the passage of the law, it becomes part of the United States Code, which is the official compilation of federal laws. The state legislatures use a similar process, in which bills become law when signed by the state's governor. Each state has its own official set of laws, some of which are published by the state and some of which are published by commercial publishers. The U.S. Code and the state codes are an important source of legal research; generally, legislators make efforts to make the language of the law as clear as possible.

However, reading the text of a federal or state law generally provides only part of the picture. In the American system of government, after the legislature passes laws and the executive (U.S. President or state governor) signs them, it is up to the judicial branch of the government, the court system, to interpret the laws and decide whether they violate any provision of the Constitution. At the state level, each state's supreme court has the ultimate authority in determining what a law means and whether or not it violates the state constitution. However, the federal courts—headed by the U.S. Supreme Court—can review state laws and court decisions to determine whether they violate federal laws or the U.S. Constitution. For example, a state court may find that a particular criminal law is valid under the state's constitution, but a federal court may then review the state court's decision and determine that the law is invalid under the U.S. Constitution.

It is important, then, to read court decisions when doing legal research. The Constitution uses language that is intentionally very general—for example, prohibiting "unreasonable searches and seizures" by the police—and court cases often provide more guidance. For example, the U.S. Supreme Court's 2001 decision in *Kyllo v. United States* held that scanning the outside of a person's house using a heat sensor to determine whether the person is growing marijuana is unreasonable—*if* it is done without a search warrant secured from a judge. Supreme Court decisions provide the most definitive explanation of the law of the land, and it is therefore important to include these in research. Often, when the Supreme Court has not decided a case on a particular issue, a decision by a federal appeals court or a state supreme court can provide guidance; but just as laws and constitutions can vary from state to state, so can federal courts be split on a particular interpretation of federal law or the U.S. Constitution. For example, federal appeals courts in Louisiana and California may reach opposite conclusions in similar cases.

Lawyers and courts refer to statutes and court decisions through a formal system of citations. Use of these citations reveals which court made the decision (or which legislature passed the statute) and when and enables the reader to locate the statute or court case quickly in a law library. For example, the legendary Supreme Court case *Brown v. Board of Education* has the legal citation 347 U.S. 483 (1954). At a law library, this 1954 decision can be found on page 483 of volume 347 of the U.S. Reports, the official collection of the Supreme Court's decisions. Citations can also be helpful in locating court cases on the Internet.

Understanding the current state of the law leads only to a partial under-standing of the issues covered by the POINT/COUNTERPOINT series. For a fuller understanding of the issues, it is necessary to look at public-policy arguments that the current state of the law is not adequately addressing the issue. Many groups lobby for new legislation or changes to existing legislation; the National Rifle Association (NRA), for example, lobbies Congress and the state legislatures constantly to make existing gun control laws less restrictive and not to pass additional laws. The NRA and other groups dedicated to various causes might also intervene in pending court cases: a group such as Planned Parenthood might file a brief *amicus curiae* (as "a friend of the court")—called an "amicus brief"—in a lawsuit that could affect abortion rights. Interest groups also use the media to influence public opinion, issuing press releases and frequently appearing in interviews on news programs and talk shows. The books in POINT/COUNTERPOINT list some of the interest groups that are active in the issue at hand, but in each case there are countless other groups working at the local, state, and national levels. It is important to read everything with a critical eye, for sometimes interest groups present information in a way that can be read only to their advantage. The informed reader must always look for bias.

Finding sources of legal information on the Internet is relatively simple thanks to "portal" sites such as FindLaw (*www.findlaw.com*), which provides access to a variety of constitutions, statutes, court opinions, law review articles, news articles, and other resources—including all Supreme Court decisions issued since 1893. Other useful sources of information include the U.S. Government Printing Office (*www.gpo.gov*), which contains a complete copy of the U.S. Code, and the Library of Congress's THOMAS system (*thomas.loc.gov*), which offers access to bills pending before Congress as well as recently passed laws. Of course, the Internet changes every second of every day, so it is best to do some independent searching. Most cases, studies, and opinions that are cited or referred to in public debate can be found online— and *everything* can be found in one library or another.

The Internet can provide a basic understanding of most important legal issues, but not all sources can be found there. To find some documents it is necessary to visit the law library of a university or a public law library; some cities have public law libraries, and many library systems keep legal documents at the main branch. On the following page are some common citation forms.

COMMON CITATION FORMS

Source of Law	Sample Citation	Notes
U.S. Supreme Court	*Employment Division v. Smith*, 485 U.S. 660 (1988)	The U.S. Reports is the official record of Supreme Court decisions. There is also an unofficial Supreme Court ("S.Ct.") reporter.
U.S. Court of Appeals	*United States v. Lambert*, 695 F.2d 536 (11th Cir.1983)	Appellate cases appear in the Federal Reporter, designated by "F." The 11th Circuit has jurisdiction in Alabama, Florida, and Georgia.
U.S. District Court	*Carillon Importers, Ltd. v. Frank Pesce Group, Inc.*, 913 F.Supp. 1559 (S.D.Fla.1996)	Federal trial-level decisions are reported in the Federal Supplement ("F.Supp."). Some states have multiple federal districts; this case originated in the Southern District of Florida.
U.S. Code	Thomas Jefferson Commemoration Commission Act, 36 U.S.C., §149 (2002)	Sometimes the popular names of legislation—names with which the public may be familiar—are included with the U.S. Code citation.
State Supreme Court	*Sterling v. Cupp*, 290 Ore. 611, 614, 625 P.2d 123, 126 (1981)	The Oregon Supreme Court decision is reported in both the state's reporter and the Pacific regional reporter.
State statute	Pennsylvania Abortion Control Act of 1982, 18 Pa. Cons. Stat. 3203-3220 (1990)	States use many different citation formats for their statutes.

111

PICTURE CREDITS

ABOUT THE AUTHOR

ALAN MARZILLI, of Durham, North Carolina, is an independent consultant working on several ongoing projects for state and federal government agencies and nonprofit organizations. He has spoken about mental health issues in over twenty states, the District of Columbia, and Puerto Rico; his work includes training mental health administrators, nonprofit management and staff, and people with mental illness and their family members on a wide variety of topics, including effective advocacy, community-based mental health services, and housing. He has written several handbooks and training curricula that are used nationally. He managed statewide and national mental health advocacy programs and worked for several public interest lobbying organizations in Washington, D.C. while studying law at Georgetown University.